Cambridge Papers in Sociology No. 5

FERTILITY AND DEPRIVATION

Published by the Syndics of the Cambridge University Press
The Pitt Building, Trumpington Street, Cambridge CB2 1RP
Bentley House, 200 Euston Road, London NW1 2DB
32 East 57th Street, New York, NY 10022, USA
296 Beaconsfield Parade, Middle Park, Melbourne 3206, Australia

© Cambridge University Press 1975

Library of Congress Catalogue Card Number: 75−2718

ISBN: 0 521 20795 9

First published 1975

Printed in Great Britain
at the University Printing House, Cambridge
(Euan Phillips, University Printer)

Contents

1
Poverty and fertility

One of the most persistent facts known to those interested in population and fertility is that the poor tend to have large families. Whilst the higher social classes are perceived as acting 'rationally' in order to limit the number of children they have – to what they can afford or can most efficiently care for – the lower class (i.e. those who have the least resources) are seen as acting 'irrationally' by having large families which they cannot afford. In the past, popular explanations of this phenomenon have been couched in terms which imply that those in the lower social class lack the 'intelligence' or the 'sense of responsibility' to engage in rational behaviour. At the present time such explanations might be given less credence, and there would be a greater willingness to accept that those in the lower social class might have different motivations or concepts of rationality from those in other social groups. However, even though high fertility is a matter of topical interest, with the current concern about questions of overpopulation, there is still a lack of research in our society which would provide an adequate understanding of high fertility among the lower working class.

In Scotland – as in Britain as a whole – those in what is usually termed the skilled-manual class tend to have a considerably smaller number of children than those in the unskilled-manual group. A desire to enquire into the sources of this variation formed the initiative for the study the findings of which are presented here. To put it simply, the question which this study aims to explore is why lower-working-class couples tend to have more children than skilled-working-class couples. The following chapters present the findings of a small-scale empirical study conducted in Aberdeen. The design of the study and the extent to which it is capable of providing an answer to the above question will be described further below.

In order to attempt an explanation of the fertility behaviour of the lower working class one must first make explicit the kind of model which one will use as the basis for formulating hypotheses about lower-working-class behaviour. Thus, before looking specifically at fertility, this chapter will examine the kinds of models which have been advanced to explain the

1

approach is distinguished by its departure from the view that societies possess a common system of values and norms to which all groups in the society adhere. It maintains that there is a separate sub-culture of poverty (which does not imply that all poor people belong to such a sub-culture). Members of the sub-culture may pay lip-service to middle-class norms but they have a separate system of values and norms which guide and help to explain their behaviour. It recognises that this culture arises from the position within the wider society of the poverty group, but states that it is reinforced by socialisation of those within the poverty group into their own system of values, beliefs and norms. The lack of integration and participation of the poor in the major institutions of society helps to reinforce, as well as explain, the existence of the culture of poverty. Some of the characteristics of the culture of poverty are, on the family level, a trend towards female-centred families, authoritarianism and low family solidarity. On an individual level there are feelings of marginality, helplessness, dependence, inferiority, lack of impulse control, present-time orientation, inability to plan for the future, a sense of resignation and fatalism, and so on. The positive aspects of the culture of poverty are particularly stressed by some authors, such as spontaneity, lack of repression, etc. As Lewis states,[8]

> 'The culture of poverty in modern nations is not only a matter of economic deprivation or disorganisation or of the *absence* of something. It is also something *positive* and provides some rewards without which the poor could hardly carry on.'

Later, however, he goes on to say that although there are positive aspects to the culture of poverty, on the whole 'it is a thin, relatively superficial culture'.

One example of an explanation of lower-class behaviour in terms of cultural factors is Miller's[9] attempt to explain lower-class gang delinquency in terms of the actor's desire to 'adhere to forms of behaviour, and to achieve standards of value as they are defined within his community'. The sort of standards and concerns of the lower class which generate gang delinquency are the high values placed upon toughness, smartness and autonomy, a concern with trouble and excitement, and a belief in fate.

8   Oscar Lewis (1966a), op. cit.

9   Walter Miller (1958), 'Lower Class Culture as a Generating Milieu of Gang Delinquency', *Journal of Social Issues*, vol. 14, pp. 5–19; Walter Miller (1968), 'The Elimination of the American Lower Class as National Policy: A Critique of the Ideology of the Poverty Movement of the 1960s', in D.P. Moynihan (ed.), *On Understanding Poverty* (Basic Books Inc., New York).

In terms of attempting to find solutions for the 'problem of poverty' then, the exponents of the culture of poverty approach would assert that improving the economic resources, widening the opportunities, etc. of such groups will fail unless any changes are congruent with the values of the culture of poverty.

The second type of model for explaining the behaviour of the lower-working-class stratum is the 'situational' one.[10] It asserts that such groups are distinguished basically by their lack of resources or social deprivation. In particular, stress is laid upon the economic position of the stratum. The important factor is seen to be a lack of generalised command over goods and services, not merely in terms of present income but taking into account their long-term wealth, skills, poverty and opportunities. Such exponents often concentrate upon the measurement of poverty in economic terms, employing such concepts as the poverty line. They may recognise that the situation of the poor may give rise to distinct norms as a means of adapting to the situation. But the important explanatory variable is seen as the situational one. Economic resources are not the only ones stressed. Examples of other relevant situational factors are, lack of educational and occupational opportunity, lack of political power (i.e. participation in decision-making), and lack of social status.[11] Three examples will serve to illustrate this approach.

'The habits of "shiftlessness", "irresponsibility", lack of "ambition", absenteeism, and of quitting the job, which management usually regards as a result of the "innate" perversity of underprivileged white and negro workers, are in fact normal responses that the worker has learned from his physical and social environment.'[12]

'Our stress is much more on cognitive and structural factors than on the more commonly cited affectual and motivational ones. The nature of the conditions of working class lives (jobs, opportunities, family structure) affects behaviour more than has been frequently realised;

10   See, for example, Allison Davis (1946), 'The Motivation of the Underprivileged Worker', in W.F. Whyte (ed.), *Industry and Society* (McGraw-Hill, New York); S.M. Miller and F. Reissman (1961), 'The Working Class Subculture: A New View', *Social Problems*, vol. 9, no. 1, pp. 86–97; S.M. Miller and P. Roby (1968), 'Poverty: Changing Social Stratification', in D.P. Moynihan (ed.), op. cit.; G. Rosenthal (1968), 'Identifying the Poor: Economic Measures of Poverty', in D.P. Moynihan (ed.), op. cit.; R.M. Titmus (1962), *Income Distribution and Social Change* (Allen and Unwin, London); H. Watts (1968), 'An Economic Definition of Poverty', in D.P. Moynihan (ed.), op. cit.

11   See S.M. Miller and P. Roby (1968), op. cit.

12   Allison Davis (1946), op. cit.

one would expect the behaviour pattern one is studying to increase or decrease as income increases or decreases. It is doubtful whether such a relationship would be found in the majority of cases of behaviour patterns which vary between the lower social class and other strata. Finally, quantifiable attributes such as low income can be found in other social classes; poverty is not necessarily confined to social class V. But the poor in other strata may not behave in the same way. This should be a question for investigation, and it should not be assumed that all 'poor' people behave in the same way and that the reason for this is solely their poverty.

Criticisms of the culture-of-poverty approach take the converse form. Fundamentally the lower working class behave as they do because they are socially (and perhaps particularly economically) deprived, and it is mis-leading to eliminate this factor from the model of explanation or to idealise the positive aspects of lower-working-class culture. Secondly, the culture-of-poverty view is that values and norms are a response to structural constraints and that is why the values of the lower working class are different from those of the wider society. However, it is possible to have values and norms that are not expressed in behaviour. People do value things which they are unable to achieve, they do hold norms which they consider they ought to adhere to if their situation were different, and they do have tastes or preferences which they cannot fulfil.[19] Such values, norms and tastes may be in line with those of middle-class strata, and thus it cannot be assumed that differential behaviour is due to differential values, etc. Thirdly, the culture-of-poverty approach tends to assume that culture is a unified integrated system. No culture is integrated to that extent and the parts change with changing circum-stances. There are some norms which are relatively resistant to change, but there are others which are ephemeral and a response to a particular situation, and which will change as that situation changes.[20]

The approach favoured in this study may be termed the 'adaptational' approach. It is in effect a combination of the culture-of-poverty view and the situational approach. It recognises that lower-working-class behaviour is an adaptation to a particular situation of deprivation (of economic resources, of opportunities for educational and occupational mobility, participation in decision-making, etc.) which is reinforced by a series of values, norms and beliefs arising from that deprived situation. Some values will be held in common with those of other strata and will guide behaviour, some will be

19   Hyman Rodman (1963), 'The Lower-Class Value Stretch', *Social Forces*, vol. 42, no. 2 (December), pp. 205–15.

20   H.J. Gans (1968), 'Culture and Class in the Study of Poverty: An Approach to Anti-Poverty Research', in D.P. Moynihan (ed.), op. cit.

consciously adhered to verbally but not followed in practice, and others will differ from those of other strata in that they are a response or adaptation to a particular situation. Behaviour should be seen as guided by a continual process of adaptation to mutually reinforcing, causally connected social dis-advantages or deprivation, which will help to produce and to reinforce a particular set of values, beliefs, norms and behaviour patterns. Although the deprivations exist in aggregate form for the lowest social class as a whole, they are not all situations ascribed to an individual at birth or during child-hood to which he can then merely passively adapt. On the contrary they are experienced in a temporal sequence throughout the individual's life, and of course not all are experienced by all individuals nor all to the same extent. However, the individual in the social class V situation has a relatively high chance of experiencing the large, poor family of origin, lack of educational opportunity, poor occupational chances, poor health, broken home, early marriage, a large number of children, a difficult housing situation, unstable marriage, unemployment, delinquency of children, arrest for criminal offences, and so on. (It should be pointed out that since the impact of such factors as these will not be the same for everybody, and will not be perceived in the same way by all, thus the values and norms which are adopted will also differ within this stratum to a certain extent.)

Other writers have recognised that neither the situational nor the cultural models on their own are adequate in attempting to explain lower-working-class behaviour. Whilst all of them recognise the importance of developing a model which utilises both types of factors, some have seen the two as exerting *independent* effects upon behaviour, whilst others — as is suggested in this study — have hypothesised the interdependence of the two sets of factors. Miller, for example, develops a typology of lower-class behaviour patterns by combining economic security or insecurity (situational factor) with familial stability or instability (cultural factor).[21] This produces a four-cell typology: for example, the 'stable poor', who are economically secure and have familial stability, and the 'strained' who have economic security but familial instability. The disadvantage of this approach is that it does not elucidate the possible relationship between familial instability and economic insecurity.

An approach closer to that suggested in this study is that adopted by Rainwater in an examination of attitudes and norms with regard to marriage,

21   S.M. Miller (1964), 'The American Lower Classes: A Typological Approach', *Social Research*, vol. 31, pp. 1–22.

Lee Rainwater, for example — while recognising the importance of situational factors — explains large families within the working class largely in terms of non-effective or non-use of birth control, which he in turns explains as being due to such factors as the lack of future orientation, the segregated conjugal role relationships, the belief that having babies is the central role of women, particular patterns of sexual behaviour, and a limited understanding of what the various birth-control methods do and what the physical aspects of conception are. Thus, he concludes (in 'Family Design'),

> 'social class is seen as exercising its influence primarily through two characteristics of the family as a social system which vary from one class sub-culture to the other: first the conjugal role-organisation, values, and practices that are characteristic of different social classes and, second, the particular role concepts and the values and practices attendant on them that are deemed appropriate for men and women in different social classes'.[28]

The situational model might, for example, explain high fertility in terms of the inability of the poor to obtain efficient contraceptive devices, either because they could not afford to purchase them or because such facilities were not made available to these groups. This model might also — in certain types of society — see children as an economic asset to the poor, because of the income they can bring into the household when they are old enough to work for a living. Thirdly, exponents of such a model might explain high fertility among the poor by seeing children as a substitute or compensation for other types of deprivation. It is not easy to find examples of the use of this type of model in fertility studies. A minor example can be found in an article by Riessman, in which she suggests that the lack of efficient use of birth control by the poor is due, not so much to the 'culture of poverty' but to the fact that public policy with regard to birth control has been confused, and services — where available — have been fragmented, inconveniently situated, inhumanely delivered and bureaucratically organised. She concludes that 'it is becoming increasingly clear that the availability of birth control facilities within lower socio-economic groups rapidly increases utilisation of these services'.[29]

The model stressing personal inadequacy would be likely to provide an explanation in terms of, for example, the lack of ability or personal stability

28   Lee Rainwater (1960), *And the Poor Get Children* (Quadrangle Books, Chicago); Lee Rainwater (1965), op. cit.

29   C.K. Riessman (1968), 'Birth Control, Culture and the Poor', *American Journal of Orthopsychology*, vol. 38 (July), pp. 693—9.

needed to understand and to pursue the practice of birth control efficiently; or it might seek an explanation in terms of children being regarded as a compensation for personal inadequacy. Such a model is implicit in the occasional popular attacks on the 'lack of control', 'fecklessness' and 'irresponsibility' of the poor. Personality characteristics have been investigated as determinants of fertility,[30] and some of them appear to fit in with such a model. Westoff et al.,[31] for example, attempt to test for a variable which they refer to as 'ability to defer impulse gratification', which 'relates to the type of psychological balance existing between impulse and self-control, that was deemed relevant to the practice of contraception'. (They do not, however, hypothesise that such a balance will be most likely to be lacking within the lower-class stratum, and their use of such a variable cannot therefore be taken as a direct application of the model under discussion here.)

The adaptational approach — as used in this study — sees the large family as a result of adaptation to the lower-class situation of deprivation, insecurity and powerlessness. It is recognised that the impact of the lower-class situation will vary between individuals or groups at any one time and with the same individual or couple over time. It is thus important to stress the fact that a variety of situational factors may need to be taken into account, and that for individual families the investigator will need to envisage a continuing and changing process of adaptation.

This process of adaptation is hypothesised as involving

(1) some general sets of norms arising out of the general situation and out of socialisation within the lower-class stratum, and

(2) some more specific sets of norms which change more rapidly as situations change.

However, many norms will be held in common with those of other strata (even if they are not adhered to in practice). Norms concerning fertility behaviour may belong to any of these three types, and should not necessarily be seen as homogeneous within the lower working class.

The process of adaptation to the lower-class situation will also involve other types of behaviour, which may or may not be normatively reinforced, but will nonetheless serve as a means of adapting to the life situation, and

30   See, for example, C.F. Westoff, R.G. Potter, P.C. Sagi and E.G. Mishler (1961), *Family Growth in Metropolitan America* (Princeton University Press); C.F. Westoff and C.V. Kiser (1958), 'The Interrelation of Fertility, Fertility Planning and Feeling of Personal Inadequacy', in P.K. Whelpton and C.V. Kiser (eds.), *Social and Psychological Factors Affecting Fertility* , vol. 3 (Millbank Memorial Fund, New York).

31   C.F. Westoff et al. (1961), op. cit.

Explanatory models for the analysis of fertility in modern industrial society have not been abundant, and have often been implicit rather than explicitly stated in fertility studies. However, most fertility studies recognise the relevance of preferences[35] with regard to family size, the efficiency of use of contraception (as well as the extent of involuntary controls on fertility), and a selection of underlying variables. Woolf, for example, states,

> 'The extent to which such ideals and expectations (i.e. with regard to family size) become a reality depends not only on the degree of control which women can exercise over their fertility but probably on a number of external factors, such as the state of the economy, for example, which might induce changes in ideals as well as in what actually might happen.'[36]

The relationships between these factors are not, however, made clear. How does a change on a macro-social level actually produce change on the micro-level of individual behaviour?

Hawthorn[37] has suggested a causal model in which the fertility of an individual or couple is seen to depend on their 'tastes' (which are largely the result of prevailing societal norms concerning appropriate family sizes) plus decisions taken by the couple concerning their preferences for combinations of competing utilities. In other words, couples weigh up the costs and benefits of children in comparison with resulting costs and benefits in other spheres. This model is similar to that developed by Easterlin[38] and Ryder.[39] Easterlin suggests that a couple embark upon the family-building process with 'a structure of preferences relating to goods, children, leisure and fertility control practices, shaped largely by prior experience'. They have to weigh these preferences against the family income potential and the prices of child care and fertility control methods relative to those of goods in general. 'The fertility record of a given household reflects this balancing of preferences against constraints over the course of the full reproductive age span.' Similarly, Ryder states,

35 Or 'ideals', 'desires' or 'expectations'.

36 Myra Woolf (1971), *Family Intentions*, Office of Population Censuses and Surveys, Social Survey Division (H.M.S.O., London).

37 G. Hawthorn (1970), *The Sociology of Fertility* (Collier-Macmillan, London).

38 R. Easterlin (1969), 'Towards a Socioeconomic Theory of Fertility: A Survey of Recent Research on Economic Factors in American Fertility', in S.J. Behrman, L. Corsa and R. Freedman (eds.), *Fertility and Family Planning: A World View* (University of Michigan Press).

39 N.B. Ryder (1959), 'Fertility' in P.H. Hauser and O.D. Duncan (eds.), *The Study of Population* (University of Chicago Press).

'The reproductive ends which couples seek to achieve by fertility regulation may be considered the consequence of a complex utilitarian calculus, involving an assessment and evaluation of the utilities and disutilities expected to flow from procreative decisions made at each copulation among desirable but competing alternatives.'

The costs which a couple take into account, he suggests, are the economic costs of a child, time, physical costs, costs of space and comfort, of emotional and physical energy, and of responsibility. The benefits he believes are less easily determined: 'in general people do not know why they want children'.

The utility model is useful in certain respects, firstly in that it emphasises the importance of studying the influence upon fertility of changes at a societal or group level, by examining the way in which such changes are converted into action by individuals or couples. Secondly, it is useful in stressing that individuals have choices to make, within the limits of a variety of constraints and that these constraints – and thus the choices also – will vary over the reproductive life span.

The utility model can, however, be criticised in a number of ways. Firstly, there is a tendency to assume that there exists in the minds of individuals a family-size 'ideal' or taste (determined by societal norms) against which individuals weigh the costs of achieving this ideal during the course of their reproductive lives. However, ideals or tastes cannot be seen as distinct from preferences which arise as a result of weighing costs and benefits. Thus, insofar as individuals make decisions as to their desired family size, the pre-vailing societal or group norms must be seen as one of the constraints or encouragements which are taken into account in reaching such decisions. Tastes are not factors to be taken as given, but as evolving and changing with the life situation of the individual. Societal norms may be perceived and internalised, and the rewards and sanctions of adhering or not adhering to them may be taken into account but they are only a part of the complex of factors which are involved in determining family-size preferences and intentions.

Secondly, utility models tend to overestimate the ability of individuals to make rational choices. If – as Hawthorn indicates[40] – 'utilities are extremely difficult to measure', then how can individuals themselves decide between x amount of one good, versus y amount of another, especially when many more than two competing goods may be involved? However, Hawthorn does stress that he is not positing total rationality on the part of all couples, but merely emphasising that they do have choices to make. Yet it should be made

40   G. Hawthorn (1970), op. cit.

than sexual intercourse without the use of birth control would produce, and a 'large' family is one which would be achieved by a fertile couple without the use of birth control. 'Effective' use of birth control here means effective in controlling family size to the number preferred.

Table 1.1 *Factors affecting the achievement of large or small families*

Achieved family size	Birth-control behaviour	Family-size preferences	Underlying variables
Small	Effective	Small family	Cultural or situational variables conducive to effective use of birth-control, and to preference for a small family
Small	Non-effective	Small family	Cultural or situational variables not conducive to effective birth-control usage, plus physical factors, etc. affecting exposure to inter-course, conception or gestation
Small	Effective	Large family	Not meaningful
Small	Non-effective	Large family	Cultural or situational variables conducive to preference for a large family, plus physical factors, etc. affecting exposure to intercourse, conception or gestation
Large	Effective	Small family	Not meaningful
Large	Non-effective	Small family	Cultural or situational variables not conducive to effective use of birth control
Large	Effective	Large family	Cultural or situational variables conducive to preference for a large family and to effective use of birth control for spacing
Large	Non-effective	Large family	Cultural or situational variables conducive to preference for a large family

Design of This Study and Method of Investigation
As previously stated the main aim of the present study is to explore lower-working-class fertility behaviour within the context of a model which lays stress on the importance of both situational and cultural factors and sees

fertility behaviour as a response to a continuing process of deprivation leading to the reinforcement of norms about the individual's powerlessness and inability to control his environment. As a study of fertility, however, the causal analysis had to begin with an examination of family-size preferences and birth-control behaviour, relating it to knowledge about and attitudes towards birth control. The major aim, however, was to be explored by interviewing a sample of married women with children and examining (a) some of the major situational areas of deprivation, insecurity, etc. through which they, their husbands and their family of procreation had passed, and (b) behaviour patterns in other spheres of social activity which are comparable to fertility behaviour in the sense that they too result from adaptation to the lower-class life situation.

This analysis would be backed up by an examination of some of the respondents' stated attitudes in relation to the general field of the individual's ability to alter his environment, and in relation to family size in particular. It should be stressed, however, that the criticisms made above of the culture of poverty model apply here – for example, the norms of middle-class society may be accepted even though they are not reflected in behaviour, or there may be norms which are accepted in one situation but which change as situations change.

It was decided that the study was to be in the nature of an exploratory examination of the subject using a small sample of respondents. It is not presumed that it will provide definitive tests of the hypotheses raised. Rather it is hoped that it will provide clues to certain tendencies and bring to light more clear hypotheses which it will then be possible to test more rigorously using either a larger or a smaller sample of respondents. We are very much aware of the fact that this is an intermediate type of study, providing neither a large enough sample to produce generalisations which can be validated through statistical analysis, nor a sufficiently intensive study to make possible a satisfactory exploration of respondents' behaviour and the meanings which underlie the statements they make. However, an intermediate study of this kind does provide insights into the factors which underlie behaviour, and also shows to what areas further research can most relevantly be directed.

It is a retrospective study using a small sample of women, once married, and all married for a similar period of time. The sample was selected from women, married in 1960/1 in Aberdeen (excluding those who subsequently left the city). The group of major interest was that where the husband was classified as being in social class V[41] at the time of the birth of the first child.

---

41   Registrar General's classification.

occupations, occupations of wife's and husband's fathers;

(7)   income, education, housing situation;

(8)   the marital relationship.

The interview took the form of going through the respondent's marriage, treating it as stages divided by the birth of each child – i.e. before the first child was born, after the first and before the second child was born, and so on. For each of these stages questions were asked on family-size preferences, birth-control behaviour, occupations, housing, etc. In this way it was felt the respondent's ability to recall events would be aided by placing each aspect of behaviour within a wider context.

Selection of Sample and Response Rate

It was hoped to interview twenty-five women in each of the four cells outlined in the previous section. In order to allow for non-response, a target sample of up to 35 women in each cell was set for selection.

From the records kept of all women delivered of at least one child in Aberdeen the names of all women married in 1960/61[47] were obtained. For those where the husband was in a social class V category at the time of the first delivery, the total number of 253 was surveyed for selection of relevant couples. For those where the husband was at that time in a social class III manual occupation (1,138), a small sample was surveyed in order to estimate how many would be applicable within the constraints of the sample required for this survey. As a result, a sample of 250 was then drawn from the 1,138, proportional to the number of first births in each year from 1960 onwards, the size of this sample being determined by the need to select 35 women with four or more children as well as 35 with two children only. This sample produced, as one would expect, more families of two children only than was required. Therefore, a selection of 35 was made on a random basis. From the 253 women in social class V only 28 had four or more children at the time of interview (as well as fulfilling the other requirements of being once married, not divorced or separated, and still living in Aberdeen), compared with 46 who had two children only. A selection of 28 was therefore made on a random basis from among that 46.

The response rates plus details of the selection of the samples are shown in Table 1.2. It can be seen from Table 1.2(b) that there was a relatively high non-contact rate in group V2. This was due to two factors: change of address which led to an inability to trace the family, or the long working hours of the wife. The relatively high refusal rate in group V4+ was also estimated as being

---

47   This is not strictly accurate, as the length of marriage data recorded on the cards was not year of marriage, but length of time married when first child was born.

Table 1.2 *Selection of sample and response rate*
(*a*) *Selection of sample*

	Social class III manual No.	Social class V No.
Total number of women married in 1960–1 and having at least one child	1,138	253
Random sample size for social class III	250	–
Number excluded (because incorrectly coded as social class III or V, not married in 1960–1, have only one or three children, twice married, moved from Aberdeen, etc.)	122	179
Number relevant to study:		
Two children only	93	46
Four or more children	35	28
Number selected for interview:		
Two children only	35	28
Four or more children	35	28

(*b*) *Response rate*

	Total No.	Total %	III2* No.	III2* %	III4+* No.	III4+* %	V2* No.	V2* %	V4+* No.	V4+* %
				Number of children within social class						
Total selected	126		35		35		28		28	
Not applicable (e.g. because couple separated, or family size incorrect, or because child died)	10		–		4		1		5	
Total applicable	116	100	35	100	31	100	27	100	23	100
Interview successfully completed	90	77	30	86	25	81	18	67	17	74
Non-contacts	16	14	4	11	4	13	7	26	1	4
Refused	10	9	1	3	2	6	2	7	5	22

* These abbreviations will in future be used to refer to the four groups of social class III or V, with 2 or 4 or more children.

due largely to two factors: suspicion of the purposes of the interview, or an inability to find the time to be interviewed at length.

Basic Characteristics of Those Interviewed

This chapter ends with a description of some of the basic characteristics of the achieved sample. They are designed merely to 'set the scene' for the analysis which follows in subsequent chapters.

The social class (in terms of the husband's occupation at the time of his wife's first delivery) and the length of time for which the sample couples have been married are already known. But although the couples have all been married for a similar length of time, one needs to determine whether they all married at approximately the same age or not. This is an important point, for age at marriage may have a considerable effect upon both the marital relationship and the family-building process. For example, age is strongly related to a woman's fecundity, and thus the earlier she marries the more capable will she be of bearing many children. The wives' and their husbands' years of birth are shown in Table 1.3. This table shows that there are differences between the groups in the age of the wife (for example those in group III2 are on average over a year older than those in the other groups). Husbands are slightly older than wives, and those with two children are somewhat older than those in the other groups. In later chapters the significance of the somewhat later marriages of those with two children will be discussed in more detail.

The question of sub-fecundity raised above was not one which this study was able to handle very satisfactorily. Women's own opinions and a reliance upon their memory of sexual behaviour and use or non-use of contraception meant that the question of the extent of sub-fecundity among the sample was extremely difficult to determine. (Total infertility due to sterilisation or hysterectomy is a different issue. This could be determined with accuracy due to access to hospital records, and the proportion of women who had had such operations will be shown below.) Only two women had ever attended the hospital for an infertility investigation (one in group III2 and one in V2). It was assumed however that the incidence of sub-fecundity would be considerably higher than that. The problem was therefore approached by calculating for groups III2 and V2 the length of time it took women to conceive when no form of birth control was being practised. It was found that these data produced a graph which reached a peak at a few months, tailed off and then rose slightly. Those women who were consistently found at this point in the distribution were therefore classified as relatively sub-fecund. This is a crude measure but after careful study of the pregnancy and birth-control histories it was decided to classify as relatively sub-fecund five

Table 1.3 *Year of birth*

	III2		III4+		V2		V4+	
	No.	%	No.	%	No.	%	No.	%
(a) Wives								
Before 1935	2	7	–	–	1	6	1	6
1935–6	6	20	1	4	2	11	1	6
1937–8	4	13	7	28	3	17	3	19
1939–40	12	40	9	36	4	22	4	23
1941–2	3	10	5	20	7	39	4	23
1943–4	3	10	3	12	1	5	4	23
Mean age in 1970	31.7		30.2		30.6		30.2	
(b) Husbands								
Before 1935	5	17	1	4	2	11	3	18
1935–6	7	23	5	20	1	6	3	18
1937–8	8	27	5	20	8	44	3	18
1939–40	8	27	11	44	4	22	2	12
1941–2	2	7	2	8	3	17	5	28
1943–4	–	–	1	4	–	–	1	6
Mean age in 1970	33.2		31.7		32.5		31.9	

women in group V2 and twelve women in group III2. Without more data however these figures must be regarded with great caution. They should be treated as an overestimation of sub-fecundity, the main advantage of which is that it can be assumed that the fecund group contains no sub-fecund women, although the relatively sub-fecund group may include women who should not be so classified. Where relevant in this report analysis will be shown separately for the fecund and relatively sub-fecund categories.

A third basic question to be asked about the sample couples is exactly how many children those with the larger families have had. As stated in an earlier section families of more than five or six live children are uncommon now in Aberdeen; thus the family-size range in this sample was narrow. Table 1.4 shows that after ten years of marriage no one in the sample had more than six children.[48]

48   See Appendix for increase in family size since the time of interview.

Table 1.4 *Number of living children*

	III2 No.	III4+ No.	V2 No.	V4+ No.
Two children	27	–	15	–
Three children*	3	–	3	–
Four children	–	20	–	10
Five children	–	4	–	5
Six children	–	1	–	2
Mean no. of children	2.1	4.2	2.2	4.5

* Those with three children are those who when selected had two children but by the time of inverview had had an additional child.

Table 1.5 gives the sex composition of these families. It shows that the majority of families include children of both sexes (71%). This is of course less likely among the two-child families than among those of a larger size; of the two-child families 55% were single-sex, whereas among the four-child families only 7% were single-sex. The significance of the sex of children for the family-building process and of the sequence in which they are born will be discussed in the next chapter.

Table 1.5 *Sex composition of families*

Number of girls in family	Number of boys in family						
	0	1	2	3	4	5	6
0	–	–	9	–	1	–	1
1	–	19	4	4	1	–	–
2	14	2	15	6	–	–	–
3	–	9	2	1	–	–	–
4	1	–	–	–	–	–	–
5	–	1	–	–	–	–	–

The total number of pregnancies experienced in order to achieve the family size shown above was of course slightly in excess of the number of living children. The ratio of number of living children to number of pregnancies shows some difference between the four groups in the sample. In group III2 only 2% of all pregnancies were 'wasted' (i.e. abortions or child deaths), in group V2 the proportion was 7%, in group III4+ 8%, and in group

V4+ it rose to 16%. These differences are due to a variety of medical and environmental factors which could not be explored in this study. The figures are shown here in order to indicate the extent of differences between the groups in this aspect of family-building experience.

A further question which may be asked about the families in this study is at what point in their marriage did they start having children, and how long a period of time was involved in the building up of their families to their present size (i.e. how long before the time of interview was the last child born). The interval between marriage and first delivery is shown in Table 1.6.

Table 1.6 *Interval between marriage and first delivery*

	III2		III4+		V2		V4+	
	No.	%	No.	%	No.	%	No.	%
Up to and including 8 months	6	20	9	36	3	17	10	59
Over 8 months, up to and including 1 year	7	23	10	40	7	39	4	23
Over 1 year, up to and including 18 months	6	20	4	16	2	11	2	12
Over 18 months, up to and including 2 years	3	10	1	4	3	17	–	–
Over 2 years, up to and including 3 years	6	20	1	4	2	11	1	6
Over 3 years	2	7	–	–	1	5	–	–

The figures show first of all a clear difference between the groups in the incidence of pre-nuptial conception (defined here as deliveries up to eight months after marriage). Those with the larger families, and particularly those in social class V, were more likely than others to have had a pre-nuptial conception. The relationship between this behaviour and subsequent family size and class position is one of the factors which will be discussed in detail in the following chapters. Table 1.6 also shows that the great majority of women had had their first child by the time they had been married for two years; only two (5%) of those with the larger families waited over two years, compared with 23% of those with the smaller families. Again a variety of questions spring from these figures: What were the reasons for the longer wait for a first child? Was it a consciously planned decision or was it the outcome of involuntary factors? These questions will also be covered in subsequent chapters.

The intervals between deliveries and the time which elapsed between the birth of the last child and the date of interview were also longer for those with two children than for those with the larger families. For example, 83% of group III2 waited over two years between the delivery of the first and second child, as did 67% of group V2, compared with only 12% of III4+ and 24% of V4+. Similarly, the time elapsing between the last delivery and the date of interview was over two years for 67% of III2, 72% of V2, 52% of III4+ and 36% of V4+. Thus, as well as controlling the number of children born in the first ten years of marriage, those with the smaller families have also achieved longer intervals between the births of their children. The questions which arise from this information are the extent to which this behaviour accorded with consciously held preferences for the size and spacing of the family, and the extent to which these outcomes were achieved by the use of contraception. An attempt to answer such questions will be made in Chapters 2 and 3.

Finally, one may ask whether the couples in this study have or have not completed building their families. It has been estimated that, in this society, the vast majority of all births have occurred by ten years after marriage.[49] One can ask women whether they wish to have more children and whether they are doing anything to prevent further births. Replies to such questions will be discussed in following chapters. At this stage will be indicated merely how many women were unable to have more pregnancies (see Table 1.7).

Table 1.7 *Whether wife could have further pregnancies at time of interview*

| | III2 | | III4+ | | V2 | | V4+ | |
	No.	%	No.	%	No.	%	No.	%
Could have further pregnancies	26	87	9	36	15	83	7	41
Could, but advised on medical grounds not to do so	1	3	1	4	–	–	–	–
Could not have further pregnancies*	3	19	15	60	3	17	10	59

* All but two of those who could not conceive another child had been sterilised; the other two had had hysterectomies.

49   Myra Woolf (1971), op. cit.

This table shows the very high incidence of sterilisation among women with four or more children, which raises a number of questions. For example, was sterilisation advised on medical grounds or did the women themselves request it? Was it seen as an alternative to other forms of birth control, and if so, why was it preferred to other methods? Again, an attempt will be made to answer these questions in other chapters.

This section has merely attempted to provide some of the background details about the families studied in this investigation. Whilst doing so it has begun to show differences between the four groups in the sample, and has raised a number of important questions. The next two chapters will cover questions concerning family-size preferences and birth-control behaviour, after which further underlying variables (both situational and cultural) will be examined.

2
Family-size preferences

It is frequently asserted that in this society, at the present time, the family-size norm lies between two and three children per married couple. However, there can be confusion between beliefs about the number of children the majority of couples desire, beliefs about the number people ought to have, and the number of children they do in fact have. It is of course true that for the past fifty years average completed family size for all marriage cohorts has remained at between two and three children.[1] Surveys also show that the majority of couples have a preference for two or three children.[2] The danger lies, however, in the popular suggestion that those who do not achieve a completed family size of two or three children are in some ways to be blamed or pitied, since it may be felt that those who have only one child are selfish because 'an only child is a lonely child' and liable to be spoiled, and that those who have more than three are 'feckless', ignorant and/or anti-social. Assumptions about family-size desires often rest upon a belief that 'preference' is a simple concept and easily capable of measurement. However, as has been stated in the previous chapter, preferences are constructed by taking into account (1) the prevailing societal or group norms (i.e. the number of children it is considered couples ought to have); (2) the family size it is considered usual to have; and (3) a complex variety of costs and benefits which couples see as the effects, for them, of a particular family size. Although it may be difficult to measure, 'preference' is nonetheless an extremely important concept in studies of causality in relation to family size. Fig. 1.1 shows how preferences can be seen as the interdependent variable in the causal chain: on the one hand as the result of a complexity of factors influencing individuals' desires and decisions, and on the other hand as an

1   General Register Office, Statistical Review of England and Wales (H.M.S.O., London); Central Statistical Office, Annual Abstract of Statistics (H.M.S.O., London).

2   See, for example, Myra Woolf (1971), *Family Intentions*, Office of Population Censuses and Surveys, Social Survey Division (H.M.S.O., London).

influence upon the use of birth control and thus upon achieved family size.

In examining family-size preferences among that group of the population which is of major interest in this study, many of the hypotheses (mentioned in the previous chapter) concerning the norms, life style and social situation of the lower class are relevant. Those beliefs and patterns of behaviour which have been hypothesised as developing as a response to the lower-class social situation are likely to affect family-size preferences in a variety of ways.

Firstly, there may be a family-size norm for that social group which differs from the norms of other social groups, and to which individuals feel they ought to conform. There may also be an assumption that there is a 'usual' preference or behaviour pattern in the group, which again may act as a constraint upon individuals' behaviour.

As well as affecting the *size* of family preferred, the lower-social-class situation may affect beliefs concerning preferences in general. Firstly, the individual may believe that it is impossible to think in terms of preferences when his life is controlled not by him but by external forces, and he himself is powerless to alter his environment. He may believe, secondly, that even though it is possible to have a preference, the connection between a preference and ensuing events is so slight that such a preference should not be taken seriously. He may even believe that if the individual makes a plan it is bound to go wrong because forces always act against his interests, and that it is better therefore not to 'tempt fate' by expressing a preference. He may also place a high positive value upon 'taking things as they come' and thus believe that one ought not to have preferences concerning some future state.

As well as affecting an individual's beliefs concerning preferences, his social situation may affect his *ability* to think in terms of preferences. He may be unable to construct rational plans for desired ends; and since his situation may often necessitate behaviour which is a series of changing responses to changing stimuli, even if he has preferences they are likely to be short-term ones which will change to accommodate changing events.

There is little doubt, however, that most people have family-size preferences however vague, ill-formulated and complex they may be. It is also likely that these preferences differ between persons and over time. One cannot assume that all people desire two or three children, and that therefore when one attempts an explanation of large families in certain groups the only thing to explain is why they have achieved *too many* children. Without some measure of preference no family-size study can determine, for example, what percentage of couples practise effective contraceptive behaviour, nor how many children are unintended or unwanted. This is the reason why, even though there are dangers of oversimplifying the measurement of preference, researchers may find that they have to accommodate such a measure

33

in order to determine other factors.

The main difficulties encountered in attempting to determine preferences for a particular number of children are as follows:

(1)   A preference may be vague or unclear and thus not capable of being verbalised, or it may not exist at all. The interview situation may, however, force an answer.

(2)   A preference can gradually become more, or less, definite.

(3)   More than one preference may be held, either simultaneously or interchangeably – for example, 'I don't want more than two if we remain in this flat, but if we move to a larger one I'd like four' (this does not necessarily mean that the respondent wants to move to a larger flat in order to have four children); or 'Sometimes I think I'd like two and sometimes I think four.'

(4)   A preference may be a mixture of attitudes difficult to resolve in order to give a numerical answer – for example, 'I'd like to have another baby to cuddle, but I don't fancy going through the birth again, and I'd like to go back to work again because we need the money. But my husband would like another, and I'd like to make him happy.'

(5)   A preference may vary in the force with which it is held. It may mean for example that there would be a sense of tragedy if the preference were not achieved, or that there would be only a sense of inconvenience.

(6)   The preferences of husband and wife are equally important in explaining family size. Husbands and wives however may hold different attitudes even when paying 'lip-service' to the preference of the other.

(7)   Preferences change over time. The amount of change varies as does the frequency with which change occurs.

(8)   A respondent may verbalise what she considers to be the norm whilst consciously (or unconsciously) not adhering to that perceived norm.

(9)   A respondent may feel under pressure to show that her preferences are in accord with the number of children she has, or expects to have.

A second type of difficulty is one that is common to all research involving interviewing. This problem is the likelihood that the researcher's rationality and the meaning which he attaches to everyday events and language may differ from those of the respondent and of the interviewer. Thus it is important to attempt to discover what the respondent understands by the questions posed by the interviewer, and the meaning attached to the answers he or she gives. In any representative sample of the population the range of meanings will be wide, and even in a restricted sample, such as the one used in this study, one cannot assume homogeneity of meaning. Cicourel[3] sums up this problem:

> 'The observer and respondent both employ methods for making the social structures of everyday life observable. The observer's task is complicated by his own use of an assumed but unstated common knowledge in entering the respondent's environment, sustaining the social relationship, posing questions, receiving answers, evaluating the respondent's environment and interpreting the findings to others. The observer must also take into account how the respondent evaluates the interviewer, the questions posed, how he formulates answers, all within the background expectancies that operate for the respondent.'

Whilst one can never know whether these problems have been overcome, one can attempt to minimise them in a variety of ways. In this study the following techniques were employed: (1) conducting at least two interviews with each respondent in order to help establish good *rapport* before the more difficult questions were asked; (2) probing as fully as possible in order to understand the meaning of a respondent's answer; (3) noting spontaneous comments either directed to the interviewer or to others who happened to be present; (4) querying any discrepancies in answers, and (5) rephrasing questions where the respondent did not appear to understand them.

Taking into account the difficulties described above and the constraints which they impose upon the study, this chapter attempts to explore to what extent the sample of women studied hold identifiable preferences for a particular number of children and what those preferences are.

Attitudes towards the number of children a couple have can be explored empirically by response to direct or indirect questions concerning family size. Indirect questions are those to assess (a) beliefs about what is happening to family size nowadays (for example, 'In general, how many children do you think people like you are tending to have nowadays?' and 'Do you think that, in general, families are larger, smaller, or about the same size as they were ten or fifteen years ago?'), (b) beliefs about family-size preferences nowadays, and (c) respondents' feelings towards the size of family people ought to have. These questions are intended to assess to what extent respondents agree that families tend to consist of two or three children, that most people have a preference for that number of children, and that they ought to have such a preference. Direct assessment of preferences was carried out by means of

---

3   Aaron Cicourel (1967), 'Fertility, Family Planning and the Social Organisation of Family Life: Some Methodological Issues', *Journal of Social Issues*, vol. 23, no. 4, pp. 57–81.

exploring respondents' own preferences with regard to the number of children they wanted at different stages of their marriage (for example, 'Did you have any ideas at that time about the number of children you'd like to have?') and by investigating the strength of preferences, the extent of agreement between husband and wife, and how preferences have changed over time, together with reasons for any change. These preferences (where visible) will be set against the number of children achieved by the respondents.

Beliefs and Attitudes about Family Size in General

The majority of those interviewed thought that people were having smaller families now than ten or fifteen years ago, and they saw the family of two or three children as the most usual situation. The main reason for the decrease was seen as the wider availability and knowledge of birth-control facilities, followed by a feeling that fewer people could afford large families nowadays.

One would expect that, if two or three children are seen as the number one ought to have, then when women are asked what constitutes a large family there will be a tendency for any number over three to be seen as a large number of children, since 'large' may be interpreted as anything above the norm. However, one would also expect the answers to be influenced by the number of children a woman has, because there will be a tendency for her to feel that there is a stigma attached to having a large family and therefore a tendency to describe her family size as 'normal' or 'not excessive'. Table 2.1 shows that no one sees less than four children as a large family, and to that extent all conform to the assumed norm, and that those with only two children are more likely than those with four or more to see four or five children as a large family. Those with four or more children are most likely to see a large family starting at six or seven children. Those in social class V with two children are somewhat more likely than those in social class III with two to see the large family starting at six or seven children. Similarly those in social class V with four or more children are more likely than those in social class III with four or more to see the large family as starting at eight or nine children. These class differences may be due to the fact that larger families are more common in social class V than social class III. With regard to the difference in answer by achieved family size, it is impossible to distinguish whether this is due to differing norms about the family size people ought to have, differences in what is seen as the most usual family size or to a rationalisation of own achieved family size.

Almost all women see one, one or two, or two children as constituting a small family. No one gives more than three as an answer to this question (Table 2.2). Again those with the larger families are more likely to state the higher number as being a small family, and those with only two children are

36

Table 2.1 *Number of children thought to be a large family*

	III2	III4+	V2	V4+
	%	%	%	%
Four/four or five	37	8	22	6
Five/five or six	40	12	44	18
Six/six or seven	10	64	28	35
Seven/seven or eight	10	8	6	6
Eight/eight or nine	3	4	–	18
Nine or more	–	4	–	18
Total	100	100	100	101
Base for percentages	30	25	18	17

Table 2.2 *Number of children thought to be a small family*

	III2	III4+	V2	V4+
	%	%	%	%
One	47	28	72	35
One or two	23	24	11	24
Two	30	40	17	35
Two or three	–	8	–	–
Three	–	–	–	6

more likely to think one child constitutes a small family. This is particularly true of those in social class V with only two children.

The next step was an attempt to discover whether there is a stigma attached to having what is thought to be either a large or a small family. If two or three children are seen as the number one ought to have, and not merely the most usual number, one might expect to see a stigma attached to having more than that number. As the small family is frequently seen as being two children one would expect the opposite of a stigma to be attached to having a small family. (If the small family is seen as one child only one might expect negative attitudes.)

Yet when respondents were asked what sort of people they thought had large families nowadays no very clear picture emerged. The answers were divided between those of a disapproving type (e.g. 'people who can't afford them', 'ignorant people'), those of an approving nature ('people with patience', 'those who like children'), and the possibly more neutral answers such as 'people who marry young' or 'Roman Catholics'. Those with the larger families are more likely, of course, to give favourable responses and those with the smaller families are likely to give the unfavourable responses, but the differences are not marked. The picture is somewhat clearer concerning the sort of people thought to have small families. Those with four or more children are more likely than those with two to say that it is those who could afford more, are selfish, or want to get ahead, and those with two children are more likely to say that it is sensible or ordinary/average people who have small families. But again the answers were widespread and there is no overriding attitude for or against large or small families.

Similarly respondents were asked what reasons they thought couples would have for wanting either four or more children or one or two children. The most common reason for wanting four or more was seen as 'liking children' (particularly among those with four or more themselves), and the most common reasons for wanting only one or two were seen as not being able to afford more, wanting to spend money on other things — such as giving children more — or couples wanting more time to themselves. Thus again there is no widespread negative attitude towards those wanting a large family, and certainly no stigma attached to those wanting only one or two children. (Only five respondents said this was due to selfishness, although this may have been implied in such answers as 'couples wanting more time to themselves'.) Woolf received a similar spread of answers when she asked a representative sample of married women who thought that three or fewer children was the ideal number for families 'without particular worries about money' why they thought some people had more than that number. Over half replied that such couples 'like children', one-third that 'they don't take precautions', and just over a quarter that 'it just happens'. Only 5.7% expressed a clearly negative attitude when they said that such couples were 'irresponsible' (although of course negative attitudes could have been implied in other answers).[4]

A series of statements used by Hill, Stycos and Back in a study of Puerto Rico was also used to assess attitudes either for or against the large or small family.[5] Their study was carried out amongst a representative sample of the Puerto Rican population during 1954–5. They used the series of statements in order to obtain some measure of consistency or ambivalence with regard to family-size preferences. Although it was realised that it would not be useful

4   M. Woolf (1971), op. cit.

5   R. Hill, J.M. Stycos and K.W. Back (1959), *The Family and Population Control* (University of North Carolina Press).

to compare their sample with the very different one used in this study, it was decided to incorporate the statements into the present study in order to provide a check on consistency of response. Each of the four statements used was delivered in a positive and negative format at different points in the interview. Respondents were asked whether they agreed or disagreed with the statements. The answers are shown in Table 2.3. As there was very little difference by social class the results are sub-divided only by size of family. The 'totally inconsistent' responses were those in which the answer to one format of the statement directly contradicted the answer to the alternative format. The 'partially inconsistent' responses were those in which the respondent answered either positively or negatively to one format of the statement, but said that she did not know to the alternative format.

This table shows that inconsistency is high. (This was also found in the Hill, Stycos and Back study, in which total inconsistency ranged from 33.1% at Statement D, to 14.8% at Statement C.) Those with two children only showed a low level of consistency of response in favour of the small family on items A and B, showing that they did not wholeheartedly support the view that small families are less trouble or that they are any happier than large families, but they were more consistent in viewing the small family as best when 'everything was considered' (item C). This may well indicate the importance they placed upon not having more children than one can afford, even though other considerations (namely the happiness of the family and the extent to which children are a trouble) did not show the small family as preferable. They were however overwhelmingly in support of the view that 'having children is one of the most important things in life' (item D).

Those with four or more children also matched those with two children in endorsing this latter statement. They differed considerably from those with small families however on the other three items: on the first two they were much less inconsistent and more overwhelmingly in favour of the large family, showing that they considered large families to be happier than small, and worth the trouble. They were however — as might be expected — likely to react inconsistently to item C or to favour the small rather than the large family. Again it appeared that questions of cost were being considered in the answers to those statements, and many of those with large families realised they would be 'better off' if they had few children.

It should be stressed that the items selected were only a sample of the range of attitudes towards having children which could have been chosen. They show however that there is an overwhelming belief in the importance of having children, but no clear-cut preference for either large or small families. The level of inconsistency is high, with 53% of the sample giving inconsistent responses to one or more of the four items selected. (Most of such

Table 2.3 *Response to statements about family size*

Statement A.   'Having many children is a burden and not worth the trouble.'

               'Having many children is a burden but it is worth the trouble.'

	Those with 2 children %	Those with 4 or more children %
Consistent in favour of small family	14	2
Consistent in favour of large family	23	72
Totally inconsistent	14	12
Partially inconsistent	36	12
Don't know	13	2

Statement B.   'The fewer the children a family has the happier it is.'

               'The more children a family has the happier it is.'

	Those with 2 children %	Those with 4 or more children %
Consistent in favour of small family	4	–
Consistent in favour of large family	31	60
Totally inconsistent	48	21
Partially inconsistent	15	17
Don't know	2	2

Statement C.   'Everything considered it's best to have few children.'

               'Everything considered it's best to have many children.'

	Those with 2 children %	Those with 4 or more children %
Consistent in favour of small family	42	29
Consistent in favour of large family	6	7
Totally inconsistent	8	17
Partially inconsistent	40	38
Don't know	4	9

Statement D. 'There are many things in life more important than having children.'
'Having children is one of the most important things in life.'

	Those with 2 children %	Those with 4 or more children %
Consistent against paramount importance of children	6	2
Consistent for paramount importance of children	75	81
Totally inconsistent	13	5
Partially inconsistent	6	10
Don't know	–	2

respondents give inconsistent responses to only one item, and there is thus no evidence that certain types of respondent always appear as inconsistent.) Also, in answer to statements A, B and C only two respondents gave answers showing total consistency in favour of small families on all three items (one each from group III2 and V2). Four respondents gave answers showing total consistency in favour of large families on all three items (one in group III2,[6] one in group III4+ and two in V4+).

The final question in this section aimed to discover whether the respondents adhered to an assumed norm of two or three children in connection with the number of children thought to be ideal for 'people like themselves' and for 'the average family'. All women were asked what they thought was the ideal number of children for the average family nowadays, and also, in case they should see one norm for most people and a different one for their own social group, what they thought was the ideal number for people like themselves.

No one said 'one' or 'one or two' children was the ideal number for the average family, so to that extent they conform to the hypothesis that one ought not to have fewer than two children (see Table 2.4). Those in social class III with two children conform most closely to the 'two or three' norm, but in the other groups four children were seen as an ideal number by between a quarter and a third of respondents. The fact that the social class V group with two children is similar to the groups with four or more children

---

6   This woman was a Roman Catholic. She believed that one should have 'as many children as God sends', and would have preferred a large family. She had a hysterectomy after the second child, for medical reasons.

Table 2.4 *Ideal number of children for the average family**

	III2 %	III4+ %	V2 %	V4+ %
Two/two or three	62	45	53	50
Three	35	5	18	—
Three or four	—	20	6	7
Four	4	25	24	36
Four or five	—	—	—	—
Five or more	—	5	—	7
Mean number	2.6	3.2	2.9	3.2

* Excluding those unable to give a definite answer.

in this respect is interesting. It may be that four children is seen as acceptable amongst social class V families and that this group of women see themselves as a special group in some ways. Nonetheless the main finding is that two, two or three, or three children is the most common attitude, even stated by 50% of those with four or more children. Yet it may be that they exclude people like themselves when they talk about the ideal for the average family. However, when asked what is the ideal number of children for people like themselves (Table 2.5) 39% of group III4+ and 50% of group V4+ still mention between two and three children. Also it is impossible to determine to what extent those who say four or more are making a rationalisation due to their achieved family size. Yet there are big differences between those with two children and those with four or more, in both social classes, in the number of children considered ideal for people like themselves.

The study of ideal family size is a common inclusion in population surveys. Unfortunately comparison is often difficult because other surveys cover different societies or periods of time, or do not sub-divide the responses by social class.[7] The most useful comparison for the purposes of this study is one which involves a prospective rather than a retrospective study, in order to determine whether the differences observed above, between those who have

7   See, for example, M. Woolf (1971), op. cit.; R. Freedman, G. Baumert and
M. Bolte (1958–9), 'Expected Family Size and Family Size Values in West
Germany', *Population Studies*, vol. 13, pp. 136–50; R. Hill, J.M. Stycos and
K.W. Back (1959), op. cit.; P.K. Whelpton, A.A. Campbell and J.E. Patterson
(1966), *Fertility and Family Planning in the United States* (Princeton University
Press).

Table 2.5 *Ideal number of children for people like themselves**

	III2 %	III4+ %	V2 %	V4+ %
Two/two or three	79	30	82	43
Three	18	9	6	7
Three or four	–	9	12	–
Four	4	43	–	36
Four or five	–	–	–	–
Five or more	–	9	–	14
Mean number	2.4	3.5	2.4	3.4

* Excluding those unable to give a definite answer.

two children and those who have four or more, are due to rationalisation after the event or not. Such a survey is being conducted by Peel[8] among a representative sample of 350 married couples in Hull. All couples were married in 1965/6 and were interviewed approximately eight months after marriage. When asked to state their ideal family size[9] the mean response for those with husbands in manual occupations rose from 3.12 children in social class III manual through 3.13 in social class IV, to 3.35 in social class V. The survey has not continued for a long enough period of time for these figures to be compared with achieved family size, but it appears that those whom past experience leads one to expect will achieve the larger families (i.e. those in social class V) have somewhat higher ideals at the start of marriage than those in other manual classes. These results lend, therefore, a certain amount of support to the view that the differences observed in Table 2.5 are real differences and not mere rationalisations.

In conclusion it appears that average family size and the ideal size is in general seen to lie between two and four children, with no overwhelming support for either the smaller or the larger size. Neither is there any high degree of stigma attached to having a large family even among those with only two children.

8   J. Peel (1970), 'The Hull Family Survey I. The Survey Couples 1966', *Journal of Biosocial Science*, vol. 2, no. 1, pp. 45–70; J. Peel (1972), 'The Hull Family Survey II. Family Planning in the First Five Years of Marriage', *Journal of Biosocial Science*, vol. 4, no. 3, pp. 333–46.

9   Peel does not state whether the question specified to whom the 'ideal' related – e.g. 'the average family' or 'people like yourselves'.

Personal Family-size Preferences

During the interview respondents were asked to talk in turn about the various time-periods in their marriage, starting with before the first child was born, up to the time since their last child arrived. For each period they were asked whether they had any ideas about the number of children they wanted then, what their husbands' ideas were, how strongly they felt as they did, and why they held those views. As has been stated above, in this study the interest lies not only in discovering whether preferences accord with achievement but whether preferences exist at all and, if they do, how frequently they change to accommodate changing circumstances. But again, as stated above, it is not easy to discover whether preferences exist nor the complexity of the attitudes involved. In the section below, however, it is hoped to give some indication of

(1)   the existence of preferences;
(2)   the number of children preferred;
(3)   the extent to which preferences accord with achievement;
(4)   whether husbands' attitudes accord with wives';
(5)   the reasons for holding a particular set of preferences and for preference change.

There are two major limitations in the study which should be borne in mind in this section:

(a)   The study was a retrospective one and therefore suffers from difficulties of recall as well as rationalisations from a present situation to that of the past. (A retrospective study may however have one advantage over a prospective study, in that it is not so likely to force an answer where no definite attitude exists — that is, it may be easier for a respondent to admit retrospectively that she had no idea how she felt at an earlier time, than — at the time — to say to an interviewer, 'I don't know.')

(b)   Interviews were conducted with wives only — unless of course husbands happened to be present. There is therefore no information on the opinions of husbands themselves, but merely on what wives thought their husbands' opinions were. However, other studies have indicated a high correlation between husbands' and wives' preferences. For example, Westoff et al. state that 'husbands present a distribution of family-size preferences similar to their wives'. They estimate that their fertility desires correlate 0.65, whilst wives' perceptions of husbands' preferences correlate 0.71 with husbands' stated preferences.[10]

---

10   C.F. Westoff, R.G. Potter, P.C. Sagi and E.G. Mishler (1961), *Family Growth in Metropolitan America* (Princeton University Press).

(1)   This section begins with the question of the existence of preferences, and how firmly they are held. If — as some have assumed — the major cause of large families is to be found in the inefficiency of some people in planning their families, then one would expect preferences to exist, and to vary little between those with large and small families. However, at marriage, only 43% of the women interviewed said they knew then exactly how many children they wanted, 27% had only a vague idea, and 30% had no idea at all. Those in social class III who now have two children were most likely to have a definite idea (54%). However, they were followed — perhaps unexpectedly — by those in social class V now with four or more children (47%) and then by social class V women now with two children (39%), with social class III women now with four or more children last (only 32% having a definite idea at that time). It is difficult to find comparable data in other studies; many surveys merely ask women how many children they would like or intend to have, rather than prefacing this question with 'Do you have any ideas about the number of children you would like to have?' Without such a preliminary question the interviewer encourages a numerical answer. Thus Thompson and Illsley report — in a prospective study of the family-building behaviour of women having their first baby in Aberdeen in 1950–3 — that only a very small proportion had no idea how many children they would prefer (at the time when they were expecting their first child) and that an additional 23% gave 'either/or' answers.[11] Peel, similarly indicates that all the couples represented in his sample were able to give a definite numerical answer to a question about their family-size intentions.[12] Yet, with careful probing, Westoff, Potter and Sagi indicated that even after women have had at least two children 'family-size preferences, like spacing preferences, are not always definite and unambiguous. In the present study 345 out of 1,165 women (30%) gave either/or responses or otherwise indicated uncertainty about their total fertility desires.'[13] There are, of course, differences between the present study and those quoted above which make comparisons hazardous — namely the differences between 'intentions' and 'preferences', and the variations in composition of the samples and the period when interviewing took place.

By the time the second child was born three-quarters of all women in this study did know how many children they wanted — group V2 was most likely to know (89%), followed by III2 and V4+ (76%), with III4+ again least

11   B. Thompson and R. Illsley (1969), 'Family Growth in Aberdeen', *Journal of Biosocial Science*, vol. 1, pp. 23–9.

12   J. Peel (1970), op. cit.

13   C.F. Westoff, R.G. Potter and P.C. Sagi (1963), *The Third Child* (Princeton University Press).

definite (68% knew how many children they wanted). At the time of interview almost all women knew how many children they preferred (this includes those who would have preferred fewer even though they accept the number they have). Eighty percent of group III2 had a firm idea, 89% of V2, 92% of III4+, and 94% of V4+. Thus preferences are not necessarily fixed at marriage, but by the time following the birth of the second child they have become fairly clear. There were only eight women who at that stage said they had no idea at all how many children they wanted. Six of them were in group III4+ and two in group V4+.

(2) The next question to be considered is the *number* of children women say they prefer, for if large families are due largely to inefficient birth-control practice then it is to be expected not only that the vast majority of women would have preferences but that they would have preferences for a small number of children. Preferences at marriage are shown in Table 2.6, distinguishing between vague and definite ideas, and between a desire for up to three children or for more than that number.

Table 2.6 *Number of children preferred at marriage*

	III2 %	III4+ %	V2 %	V4+ %
No definite idea	13	32	50	29
Vague idea — up to 3 children	24	28	11	18
— 3 or 4 or more	10	8	—	6
Definite idea — up to 3 children	50	20	28	41
— 3 or 4 or more	3	12	11	6

At this early stage in the marriage there were few women who wanted more than three children (although there were still many who had no idea). It is interesting that only a small minority of those who went on to achieve four or more children expressed a preference for a large family when they first got married. The definite desire for a small family is particularly marked in group V4+. Confidence in these findings is increased by (1) the fact that those women who achieved large families do not appear to have rationalised their behaviour by bringing their initial preferences into line with their achievement, and (2) by the findings of other prospective studies. Thus Thompson and Illsley found that 75% of women interviewed when expecting their first child wanted no more than three children. For those who, after ten years, had achieved only one child the proportion was 79%, for those who achieved two it was 76%, for those with three it was 67%, and for those who achieved four or more it was as high as 81%.[14]

The implications of Table 2.6 are that if family-size preferences have not changed since early marriage then it is largely inefficient or non-use of birth control, rather than desires, which accounts for large families. However, as will be shown below, for a large number of women a change of mind did occur, or ideas became more definite, with regard to the number of children desired.

If one examines women's preferences after the first child was born it appears that there has been little change since the time of the marriage except among those in group V2. In groups III2 and III4+ similar proportions were undecided but there was a slight decrease in the small proportions wanting more than three children, there were no changes in group V4+, but in V2 the proportion wanting up to three children had increased to 72% and the percentage undecided had dropped to 22%. (Immediately after the first child was born many women said that they felt they wanted no more children because of the experience of giving birth, but that this feeling soon passed and they reverted to former preferences.)

According to the women interviewed, after the second child was born preferences had changed slightly — mainly in the direction of becoming more definite. Nearly all women had some idea how many children they wanted even though it might be only a vague idea. There were still only few preferences for the larger family even among those who at interview had four or more children. Thus 92% of those who at interview had two children wanted one, two, two or three, or three children after their second child was born. Only 8% wanted more than that. For those now with four or more children, the equivalent proportions were 60% and 21% respectively (19% still had no definite ideas).

To sum up, therefore, between marriage and the time after the birth of the second child there was a gradual process of family-size preferences becoming more definite, mainly in terms of a preference for a relatively small family; the proportion wanting larger families remained small. (It declined slightly in groups III2 and V2, remained the same in III4+, and increased very slightly in group V4+.)

When one turns to family-size preferences at the time of interview, the picture has changed considerably for those with four or more children, but not at all for those with only two. The number expressing a preference for the larger families has remained the same for those with only two children,

14   B. Thompson and R. Illsley (1969), op. cit. Unpublished data from the study of 'family growth in Aberdeen' have been analysed in order to provide some of the additional findings quoted here.

Table 2.7 *Comparison between number of children preferred at marriage and at time of interview**

(*a*) *Those with an achieved family size of two children*

Number preferred at marriage	Number preferred at interview							
	One	Two	Two or three	Three	Three or four	Four	Five	Six
One	**1**							
Two	1	**13**	1	1				
Two or three	1	2	**1**					
Three			3	**2**				
Three or four				1				
Four		1				**3**		
Five								
Six			1					
Small family		2		1				
No idea	1	7	2	2		1		
Total	4	25	8	7	–	4	–	–

but has risen to just over a half for those with four or more children. Comparisons between the preferences which the women said they had when they got married and those which they now hold are shown in Table 2.7. The figures are shown separately for those who have achieved either the smaller or the larger families, but the two social classes are combined, since very little difference was observed between them.

Extrapolating from Table 2.7 it can be seen that 34% of those with four or more children have increased their preferences since they got married, compared with only 4% of those with two children. Twenty-one percent of this latter group have experienced a decrease in preferred family size, compared with only 7% of those with four or more children. The preferences of those with only two children are also more likely to have remained constant (42%) than are those of the women with four or more children (21%). For those whose preferences have become more definite, all but one of those with two children have formulated desires for between one and three children, whereas those who have achieved four or more children are more likely to have decided that they would prefer four or more children.

These results are undoubtedly due partly to a rationalisation after the event, but the process of interviewing indicated — as far as possible — that in

(b) *Those with an achieved family size of four or more children*

Number preferred at marriage	Number preferred at interview									
	One	Two	Two or three	Three	Three or four	Four	Five	Five or six	Six	Inconsistent
One						1				
Two		5		5		5				
Two or three		1	1	1	1					
Three				2						
Three or four										
Four						3	1			
Five										
Five or six										
Six or more						2			1	
No idea				4		5	1	1	1	1
Total	–	6	1	12	1	16	2	1	2	1

* This table does not take into account whether preferences were vague or definite, or whether or not the respondent said she accepted the number of children she had, even though she would have preferred a different number. In such cases it is the number preferred, rather than the number accepted, which is given in this table.

many cases this did not appear to have occurred. Attitudes were checked against behaviour and inconsistencies were questioned, and as some of the examples given below (section 5) will show, there often appeared to be a real change in preferences.

The extent of preference change found in this study cannot be compared closely with the findings of other surveys, since there are no strictly comparable data. However, there are some findings which are in line with those reported here. For example, it was found in this study that 25% of those with two children said they had experienced a definite increase or decrease in family-size preference between marriage and time of interview, compared with 41% of those with four or more children. Both Peel[15] and Thompson and Illsley[16] found that just over 40% of their samples had experienced an equivalent change after five years of marriage. One would expect the proportion experiencing change in this sense to be higher in these two studies than in the present investigation because both samples contained fewer respondents who were uncertain about their preferences at the start of their married life. If such women are excluded from the present study, the proportion experiencing change in preferences rises to 38% for those with two children and 59% for those with four or more children. A difference between those who achieved either the smaller or the larger families was also found by Thompson and Illsley — namely that 40% of those with up to two children had experienced definite change in preferences compared with 51% of those with three or more children.

(3)   Since the aim of this chapter is to demonstrate to what extent differential family size is due to differential preferences it is important — having outlined preferences and preference change — to show to what extent achieved family size has matched preferences. If preferences closely match achieved family size, then what has to be explained is why preferences differ. If however there is a discrepancy between preferences and achievement then one must ask why some women have more or fewer children than they want.

The question of whether respondents had more, fewer, or about the number of children they wanted was calculated not simply by asking them how many children they wanted at the present time, but by talking with them about the time-period between the birth of each of their children and how they had felt then. For example, if a woman stated that after her nth child she had felt that that was enough, and if when she became pregnant again she had wished it had not happened again at all, then n children was counted as being the number she now preferred, even if she said later in the interview that 'you accept them once you've got them'. The results are shown in Table 2.8. There was no significant difference between social classes when family size was held constant, and the two class groups have therefore been combined. Even though the preferences of those with four or more children, at the time of interview, showed a higher proportion wanting three or four or more children than those with only two children, the women are still much more likely than those with only two to have achieved more children than they would have preferred. Even where women do want the

15   J. Peel (1972), op. cit.

16   B. Thompson and R. Illsley (1969), op. cit.

Table 2.8 *Whether respondent has achieved the number of children she would prefer, at time of interview*

	Those with 2 children (%)	Those with 4 or more children (%)
Respondent has		
− Number of children she now wants	56*	36*
− More children than she wants	10	55*
− Fewer children than she wants	17*	7
Inconsistent views†	17	2

* This group includes one respondent pregnant at the time of interview.
† An example of an inconsistent view is 'Sometimes I think I've got enough but at other times I think I'd like another one.'

larger-size families their preferences are not for a very great number of children (see Table 2.7b). The following are some typical examples of the viewpoints of those with more children than they wanted;

> 'Four was the absolute deadline − it's the bringing them up that's the problem − You need enough money to go round.'

> 'I was happy with four but I didn't want any more. I wanted to get sterilised but they said I was too young. I was worried about being able to cope with them all.'

> 'I felt four was O.K. but no more − It was the money side of it really − and I used to lose my patience, I was so tired.'

Again it is difficult to find comparative data from other studies. For example, in some studies comparisons are made between 'ideals' and achieved family size, whilst in others achieved family size is compared with the number of children wanted at marriage or after five years of marriage. However all studies show a discrepancy between number of children preferred (however defined) and number achieved. For example, Woolf states:

> '73% of married women with four or more children had more children than considered ideal for families like themselves and a further 5% although not in excess of their ideal said they had not wanted their last child.'[17]

17   M. Woolf (1971), op. cit.

Thompson and Illsley found that

'After ten years of parenthood, 14% of women had fewer children than they had stated a preference for at 5 years. An even larger proportion (23%) had more children than they had wanted and this included all the women with 5 or more children.'[18] (In the present study nine out of the twelve women with five or more children felt they had more than they would have preferred, two had the number they wanted, and one had fewer than she wanted.)

(4)   Before going on to discuss why respondents felt they held particular family-size preferences, and why preferences changed, it is appropriate at this stage to consider the family-size desires of respondents' husbands (as reported by their wives), to examine the extent of agreement or disagreement, and whether it varies from group to group. For if, for example, husbands' preferences are seen to be closer to achieved family size than wives', then this factor must be taken as an important interdependent variable in the attempted explanation of differential fertility.

Firstly, it is important to discover whether husbands and wives talked about their family-size preferences with one another, for if they did not it is less likely that they could have influenced one another's preferences or behaviour in relation to family size, except of course in an implicit manner. At the time of marriage the proportion of couples who were perceived by the wives as having talked about the number of children they wanted was approximately a third in all groups except III2, where it was just over half. Others talked together about wanting children but not specifically about the number wanted. Only about a third of the couples in groups III2 and V2 were perceived as not having talked about the subject at all, whereas 45% of group III4+ and 53% of V4+ did not think they and their husbands talked about having children at that time. By the time after the second child was born, all but 17% of the wives now with only two children thought that they and their husbands had discussed the number of children they wanted. At that stage (i.e. after the second child was born) 38% of those who now have four or more children had not discussed it. Yet by the time the fourth child had been born all but two of this group had — in their estimation — talked about the subject with their husbands. Thus only a very small minority of couples were seen as never having discussed the number of children they wanted. In nearly every one of these cases the wife said that the husband left it up to her and did not worry about it. It should be added that even when couples

18   B. Thompson and R. Illsley (1969), op. cit.

did not discuss the matter, the majority of wives felt they knew what their husbands thought. It should also be noted that 'talking about' the subject meant a variety of different things, from a long serious discussion about how the couple felt and what they should do, to a few passing remarks on the subject in the course of general conversation.

When one turns to the question of whether husbands and wives agreed or disagreed in their preferences, it is clear that the complexity of the subject makes comparison difficult. Over a ten-year period of marriage, both husbands' and wives' preferences may change and it is unlikely that they will be in agreement at all times. However, for each of the time-periods studied, wives stated that they and their husbands were in agreement at each time-period in just over 50% of the cases in groups III2 and V2. In group III4+ about one-third of wives felt that they and their husbands had been in agreement at each time-period, whereas in V4+ only two out of the seventeen wives felt this to be true. Table 2.9 shows the extent of similarity of preferences between husbands and wives (as perceived by the wives) at the time of interview.

Table 2.9 *Similarity of husband's and wife's family-size preferences at time of interview*

	III2 %	III4+ %	V2 %	V4+ %
Husband would now prefer:				
− Same number of children as wife	60	52	61	29
− More children than wife	10	28	6	29
− Fewer children than wife	13	12	11	29
Husband has no definite ideas	10	8	17	6
Wife does not know husband's preferences	7	−	6	6

Table 2.9 shows that those couples who have two children only are seen as being in agreement over preferences more frequently than those with four or more children (particularly more than those in group V4+). Yet this table does not show whether the husband is more or less likely to have achieved the number of children he would prefer than the wife. These figures are given in Table 2.10, which shows that it is more likely in families with two children that both the husband and the wife have achieved the number of children they wanted, than in families with four or more. In the larger families it is more likely that neither the husband nor the wife has achieved the number of children he or she would have preferred. Yet in these larger families it is also

53

Table 2.10 *Comparison between husband and wife on the question of whether or not they achieved the number of children preferred, at time of interview*

	Those with 2 children %	Those with 4 or more children %
Both achieved number wanted	40	24
Neither achieved number wanted	19	38
Husband achieved number wanted, but not wife	6	21
Wife achieved number wanted, but not husband	8	7
Husband's views inconsistent/doesn't mind/ wife doesn't know his preferences	21	7
Wife's views inconsistent	6	3

somewhat more likely — in the wife's estimation — that the husband has achieved the number of children he wanted than that the wife has (i.e. 45% of husbands had the number of children they wanted compared with only 31% of wives). Thus it appears that there are some cases in which the views of husbands may have overridden those of their wives and have had an important influence upon achieved family size. This pattern appeared strongly in certain cases.

For example, there was a family with five children, in which after the fourth child the wife said she had 'thought that was quite enough to look after and as many as we could afford'. But, she added, 'we only had one boy and my husband thought he might turn out sissy if he didn't have the company of a brother'. The husband 'kept on about wanting another boy'. Eventually they did have another child, which was a second boy, and after that the wife was sterilised.

Another example was a family of four children, in which the wife stated that she had really wanted to stop having children after the third. She had wanted a third child because the first two were boys and 'I wanted my girl.' The third child was however another boy, but the wife said she still felt that was quite enough to cope with. However, she reported that ever since she and her husband had got married he had said that he wanted four children. 'He came from a big family and they were a happy family, and he was determined to get his four. We disagreed about it — but not violently. There's no point in that — If you're meant to have four you will.' They did have a fourth child, after which the wife went on the pill ('I at last got my husband to agree to it').

54

(5) The final section of this chapter concerns reasons for holding particular preference sets and for preference change. Before entering into this discussion a few words of caution should be expressed about the interpretation of the data on preferences and preference change. There is no doubt that the survey showed that it is legitimate and meaningful to talk in terms of respondents' preferences. But it is clear that in many cases the data have had to be simplified from the often lengthy and complex statements made by respondents in the interviews. Whilst care has been taken to avoid bias, a few examples of answers to questions about preferences will help to show more clearly the complexity of attitudes.

Respondent talking about her feelings after her first child was born:

> 'I didn't want any more but when she was about eighteen months I said I'd like another — but I also said I didn't want another, because I hated the idea of going into hospital to have it.'

Respondent talking about how she felt after she had two children:

> 'We think we're just fine now — although sometimes I think I'd like another, and I wouldn't like to think I'll never have another — but moneywise I think we're just fine.'

Respondent talking about the time after she had her third child:

> 'I was happy with three — but I also wanted another — to make my husband happy.'

Respondent talking about how she felt when she had four children:

> 'I didn't want any more because I was worried about being able to cope.'

Then she added,

> 'but the more you have the easier it seems to cope with them'.

Respondent talking about how she felt after she had three children:

> 'I didn't think I wanted any more but at times I did want another because I felt lost without a baby — my nerves are better when I have a baby — I love kiddies — and as well I wanted to try for a boy.'

Respondent talking about the time after she had her second child:

> 'We think two is enough financially, but if we get another we'd be quite happy — if the second one hadn't been a boy we'd definitely have had another.'

There are two distinct questions to be answered in this section, namely the reasons for holding a particular preference, and the reasons for change. Both involve similar types of answer and are hard to disentangle at the analysis stage.

Before presenting the findings one further point should be mentioned. This is the importance of distinguishing the difference between conscious reasons (i.e. the answers given by respondents in the interview), unconscious reasons, and causes (which may involve reasons, but may also involve the factors which influence reasons, or other factors which affect behaviour but of which the individual is unaware). Here attention is confined to the reasons given by respondents when discussing their family-size preferences. In the chapters which follow it is hoped to shed further light upon the question of the causes of differential fertility.

Table 2.11 summarises the sort of reason given to explain the number of children respondents thought they wanted to have when they got married. There was of course a wide variety of answers, although they all seemed to reflect the conventional beliefs about the reasons for wanting a particular number of children. They fall on the whole into two types of answer – the reasons for wanting as many as the number stated (more often given by those who wanted four or more children), and the reasons for not wanting more than the number stated (confined to those who wanted less than four children). For example, many women stated that they wanted two children at that time because they thought that would be as many as they could afford, whereas others said they wanted two because one child would be lonely or become spoiled. The main reason for wanting the smaller-size family was undoubtedly financial, followed by the desire not to have an 'only' child. For those wanting the larger families there was no one overriding reason. Table 2.11 is broken down by size of family preferred, and not by social class or size of family achieved since there appeared to be little difference in terms of such groupings.

By the time of interview – as shown in an earlier section – many family-size preferences were perceived as having changed or become more definite (see Table 2.7). Of course, by comparing only preferences at marriage and at time of interview, a great deal of preference change is concealed. For example, a respondent may change her ideas one or more times and then revert to her preference at time of marriage. However, comparing merely the preference at marriage with the preference at interview, one can see a greater likelihood of change amongst those who now have four or more children than among those with only two. The former are also more likely to have experienced an increase rather than a decrease in their preferences (see Table 2.12).

56

Table 2.11 *Main reasons given for family-size preferences at time of marriage*

	Number of children preferred*					
	Small no./ one/two		Two or three/ three		Four or more	
	No.	%	No.	%	No.	%
Reasons expressed in terms of explaining why respondent did not want more than no. stated						
— Reasons mainly involving benefit to parents (e.g. felt it was enough to cope with)	6		3		–	
— Reasons mainly involving benefit to children (e.g. felt they would receive more attention)	2	48	1	39	–	–
— Other/either (e.g. financial reasons)	16		5		–	
Reasons expressed in terms of explaining why respondent wanted as many as no. stated						
— Reasons mainly involving benefit to parents (e.g. respondent likes children)	2		1		3	
— Reasons mainly involving benefit to children (e.g. they would not be lonely, spoiled)	12	30	3	26	5	71
— Other/either (e.g. the family would be happier)	1		2		4	
Other reasons						
— Just seemed a nice no./ ideal no./enough	6		4		5	
— Other	1	22	2	35	–	29
No particular reason/don't know	4		3		–	

* Combining 'vague' and 'definite' preferences.

Table 2.12 *Direction of change in family-size preferences between marriage and time of interview*

	Those with 2 children %	Those with 4 or more children %
Preferences stated as being similar at both time-periods	42	29
Preferences higher at interview than at marriage	4	33
Preferences lower at interview than at marriage	21	7
Preferences indefinite at marriage — by interview preferred up to 3 children	31	10
Preferences indefinite at marriage — by interview preferred 4 or more children	2	19
Other	–	2

Rainwater provides some evidence which is in line with the findings presented here. In his study of fertility among a sample of American couples he found the following picture of preference change.

'In sharp contrast to the lower-middle class in which as many as one-third of the respondents revised their initial expectations *downward*, and the upper-middle class, in which few men and women changed their initial expectations at all, about one-third of the lower-lower class women had shifted in the direction of larger families.'

Although he does not analyse these findings by achieved family size, he does show earlier that there is a clear inverse relationship between social class and achieved family size.[19]

The reasons for revising family-size preferences either upwards or downwards were of course often complex. In this study respondents who had experienced a decrease in preference found it easier to give reasons than those whose preferences had been revised upwards. Of the twelve women who stated that they had decreased their preferences since the time when

19   L. Rainwater (1965), *Family Design: Marital Sexuality, Family Size and Contraception* (Aldine Publishing Co., Chicago).

they got married, seven mentioned financial reasons. For example,

> 'When we got married I thought I'd like to have about four children —
> because I love kiddies. It wasn't until after I'd had one that I realised
> how expensive they are to keep. When we got two I thought that was
> our lot — it was as many as we could afford to look after and keep nice.'

Another common reason was the question of the amount of time and energy
involved in caring for children. Such respondents mentioned their awareness
of how much 'children tie you down', or how they realised that they 'had
enough to cope with'. Also mentioned by two respondents was the fact that
the first two children had been one of each sex, which had made them feel
that they need not go on to have more children.

This picture is again supported by the findings of other studies. Peel, for
example, found that the four main reasons for decreasing family-size intentions, after five years of marriage, were — in order of frequency —
'economic' (52%), 'health' (19%), 'hard work involved' (10%) and 'achieved
one of each' (8%).[20] (The fact that 'health' is a more important factor in his
study than in the present one is probably due to differences in the nature of
the samples.)

Rainwater also noted the importance of financial reasons and the ability
to 'cope with' children.

> 'On the surface, the most compelling reason for reducing initial
> aspirations is financial — some couples find the medical expenses of
> having children hard to bear, others are worried by gradually mounting
> costs as each additional child requires clothes, food, recreation and
> education. But behind these easy justifications for reducing initial
> aspirations is a factor that often pinches even more . . . These people
> come to believe that having as many children as they initially wanted
> would be a psychological burden of demands, emotional control,
> attention, and giving which they would find difficult to manage.'[21]

Those who revise their family-size preferences upwards are very different
from those who revise them downwards. There were seventeen respondents in
the present study whose preferences increased between marriage and time of
interview, excluding those who said they had not wished for another child
but 'accepted him once we'd got him'. Three-quarters of those women who
had more children than they would have preferred said that they accepted

20   J. Peel (1972), op. cit.
21   L. Rainwater (1965), op. cit.

them once they had got them. If one includes rather than excludes these amongst those whose preferences have increased, such acceptance after the event becomes the main reason for preference increase. This was also found by Rainwater and Peel in the studies quoted above. Peel states that 'the biggest single reason for upward revaluation of intended family size was un-intentional over-achievement'. And Rainwater concludes that 'in the majority of cases, passive acceptance of a string of children is more apparent than active choice or wish'.

However, this section is more concerned with active preference increase than with passive acceptance. As stated earlier, many of the respondents found it difficult to explain why they wanted more children than they said they had expressed a preference for earlier in their marriage. There was however one factor which was mentioned by seven out of the seventeen, and this was a desire to 'try for' a child of the sex not yet represented among their children. After 'unintentional over-achievement' Peel also lists this as the most important reason for increase in intentions. Also, Westoff et al. — in their study of American couples with two children — state that their data 'provide unequivocal evidence of a relationship between sex of offspring and the number of additional children desired. On the average couples having children of the same sex desire the most children.'[22]

It is thus worth examining whether in fact those in groups III4+ and V4+ are more likely than those in the other two groups to have had the first two children of the same sex. The position is shown in Table 2.13. The differences between the groups are not marked: groups III2 and III4+ are almost equally likely to have had two children of the same sex, and although group V2 is slightly more likely than V4+ to have had two of a different sex the differ-ence between them is not great.

What is in need of explanation therefore is why some women with two children of the same sex feel that they would like to 'try for' another of a different sex, whereas others decide that two children is enough even though both sexes are not represented. However, since the sex of the first two children was not a factor which appeared to help account for differential fertility in this study, the question was not explored further.

Apart from the desire to have a child of a different sex, other reasons for an increase in family-size preferences were extremely diverse, each one being supported by only one or two of the seventeen respondents whose prefer-ences had increased. Some examples of the diversity are shown below:

22   C.F. Westoff, R.G. Potter, P.C. Sagi and E.G. Mishler (1961), op. cit.

Table 2.13 *Whether first two live children were of the same sex* *

	III2	III4+	V2	V4+
	%	%	%	%
First two children				
— Of same sex	63	60	40	47
— Of different sexes	37	40	60	53

* Omitting those respondents in III2 and V2 (3 in each group) who had a third child by the time of interview.

> 'With three there's always one that's left out, so I thought I'd like to bring it up to the even number — and one more makes no difference.'
>
> 'My husband was in a steady job by then — so we thought we would afford another one.'
>
> 'I had to work while my first two were babies — My mother really saw them through the baby stage. When I didn't have to work I wanted another baby — so I could look after it myself.'
>
> 'I just love having a baby around.'
>
> 'My husband had a nervous breakdown — We thought another baby might help.'

One further question concerning strength of feeling about achieved family size may add to the picture outlined in this chapter. This was a question in which women were asked what differences they felt it would make if they had had either two fewer or two more children than they already have. (Those with only two children were asked first what difference it would make if they only had one child.) Table 2.14 summarises the answers by dividing them into those which stressed either the beneficial or adverse effects for either the children or the parents. Examining first those with two children only, it is clear that the majority of respondents felt that it would neither be a good thing to have more children nor to have fewer children. For most of these couples a smaller family would have meant only one child, and the beliefs about 'only' children being lonely and/or spoiled were strongly evident. If there were two more children in the family the adverse effects on the parents were mainly seen to be financial worries, an inability to cope, or the fact that the respondent would have less freedom. The adverse effects on the children were mainly seen to be that they would get less attention or less materially.

For those with four or more children, the majority felt it would not be a

Table 2.14 *Difference respondent felt it would make if she had either two more or two fewer children**

	Those with 2 children %	Those with 4 or more children %
(a) *Two fewer children*†		
Beneficial effect for parents	4	26
Beneficial effect for children	4	19
Adverse effect for parents	10	10
Adverse effect for children	67	10
No difference/hardly any difference	17	31
Other answers	6	10
Don't know	4	5
Base for percentages	48	42
(b) *Two more children*		
Beneficial effect for parents	2	–
Beneficial effect for children	6	–
Adverse effect for parents	54	64
Adverse effect for children	33	14
No difference/hardly any difference	19	29
Other answers	10	5
Don't know	2	–
Base for percentages	48	42

* Percentages add to more than 100 because some respondents gave more than one answer.

† Those with two children were asked what difference it would make if they had only one child.

good thing to have more children, but there was less agreement on the effects of having two fewer children. Nearly a third of those respondents felt it would make no difference or hardly any difference if they had two more children, and a similar proportion thought that it would make no difference if they had two fewer children. But two-thirds thought there would be an adverse effect for the parents if the family were larger. Many of them expressed this feeling very strongly, saying 'I'd go crazy', 'I'd have a breakdown' or even 'I'd take my life.' A quarter thought it would be a good thing from the parents' point of view if the family were smaller, and a fifth that it would be a good thing from the children's point of view. The sort of answers given were that they would be able to 'cope' better, they would be better off financially or that the children would get more attention or more materially. One in ten thought it would have an adverse effect on the parents if there were two fewer children, and a similar proportion thought such a situation would have an adverse effect upon the children. These respondents tended to think that the parents would be lonely with a smaller family or that the children would be lonely or become spoiled.

The results of this question therefore support the finding that the majority of those with two children have the number of children they want (neither too many nor too few), whereas whilst the majority of those with four or more children would not like more, they are somewhat divided over whether it would have been preferable to have had a smaller family. Because many of them have had to accept more children than they would have preferred, they have undoubtedly developed reasons why fewer children would have been less preferable (or no more preferable) than the number which they have achieved.

It has now been shown that preferences about the number of children wanted do emerge and become more definite as a marriage continues and as more children are born. It has also been found that although those with four or more children at interview are more likely than those with only two children to want more children, they are also even more likely to have achieved a greater number of children than they would have preferred. The difference between the two groups therefore − in terms of family size − is partly explained by differences in preferences. But a greater difference is to be found in the ability or inability to control family size to the number of children preferred. As Whelpton et al. state, 'lower status couples do not have more children than higher status couples simply because they want more' but because of 'a relatively high prevalence of severe excess fertility in the lower education and income groups'.[23]

In this chapter very little difference was found between the two social classes when family size was held constant. The preferences, preference change, reasons for preferences and the extent of agreement between preferences and achieved family size were very similar for those in either social class with only two children and for those with four or more children. However, this does not mean that the social-class distinctions can be abandoned; as will be shown in following chapters, the explanations which can be found for the factors described in this chapter do differ to some extent by social class.

23   P.K. Whelpton, A.A. Campbell and J.E. Patterson (1966), op. cit.

The reasons for the differences in women's preferences have been examined in relation to their own feelings about why they wanted a particular number of children, and it has been shown that, whilst there is a wide diversity of opinion, financial considerations, feelings about the ability to cope with children, and a desire to have both sexes represented figure highly among the expressed reasons. A variation in preference between husband and wife appears in a minority of cases to be a significant element to be taken into account in explaining differential family size. However, the question of whether or not the first two children were of the same sex does not appear to be relevant. It is hypothesised that other factors which may influence differential preferences are differing attitudes towards birth control, differing goals or ambitions, or differing beliefs or values about the individual and his control over his environment. These factors will be examined in greater detail in the following chapters.

3
Birth control: knowledge, attitudes and behaviour

Family-size Limitation and Spacing of Births

It has been shown in the previous chapter that although women with large and small families differ in terms of the number of children they would prefer to have, this factor alone cannot account for the differences in family size between the two groups. Table 2.8 shows that 56% of those with two children have the number they wanted whereas the same is true of only 36% of those with four or more children. Similarly 55% of those with four or more children have more children than they would have preferred, compared with only 10% of those with two children.[1] In many cases therefore the differences in family size must result from more effective use of birth control[2] among those with small families (except in cases of relative sub-fecundity) than among those with four or more children. This chapter will demonstrate the truth of this hypothesis, and will also attempt to show that there is a relationship between less effective or non-use of birth control and a lack of knowledge about the more efficient methods of contraception, plus less favourable attitudes towards the use of contraception.

Effectiveness of birth-control practice is not of course a dichotomous variable: people are not either effective or non-effective birth-control users. It is possible to postulate the kinds of behaviour which constitute the upper and lower ends of the spectrum. A couple at the upper end of the spectrum would be one that wished for fewer children than sexual intercourse without birth control might produce, used an efficient method of contraception when they did not wish for a pregnancy, and managed to achieve their desired number of children with the desired interval of time between each one. A couple at the lower end of the spectrum would use no form of birth control and would achieve more children than they preferred, with shorter time

---

1   The difference between the two groups in this respect is significant at the 0.1% level (chi-squared = 17.9, with two degrees of freedom).

2   'Birth control' here includes abstinence from sexual intercourse, termination of pregnancy, and sterilisation.

intervals between them than they would have liked. There are, of course, some couples who cannot be allocated to a position along such a continuum; there are those who have no definite ideas about the number of children they want, and one therefore has no yardstick by which to measure the effectiveness of their birth-control practice; there are those couples who achieve the number of children they want, at the desired intervals, without the use (or with inefficient use) of birth control; conversely there are those who have made rational use of the possibilities of birth control available to them and yet have achieved more children than they would have preferred.

Because of the problems of measurement, the extent of effectiveness of birth-control use can be only crudely expressed. In Table 3.1 an attempt is made to show the number of women who can be called effective in terms of their attempts both to limit the number of children and to space them as they desired. Effectiveness is here taken to mean firstly effectiveness in the limitation of children to the number now wanted (i.e. at the time of interview). Secondly effectiveness of spacing is taken to mean that at the time of each conception the respondent wanted to become pregnant and was glad that she got pregnant when she did rather than earlier or later. It does not necessarily mean that she and her husband gave up birth control in order to get pregnant. They may not have used birth control at all, because they wanted a child 'straight away'. This is therefore an introductory set of figures, which give no information about the number of couples who practised birth control, although of course some inferences can be made. Section (b) of Table 3.1 is similar to (a) except that those women who have been classified as relatively sub-fecund[3] are excluded from analysis. This cuts down slightly the proportions with fewer children than they wanted and those with the number of children they wanted, but otherwise has little effect upon the proportions. The table shows that there is hardly any difference between those with four or more children in social class III and those with four or more children in social class V. Group V2 has the highest proportion of respondents with both the number of children they now want and with the spacing between the children as they wanted it (eight out of the eighteen), followed by group III2 (six out of thirty). Only one person with four or more children can be counted as being an effective limiter and spacer, and that is due only to the fact that she and her husband rarely used contraception and gladly accepted each child as it appeared.

In terms of limitation only (excluding spacing) the proportions of women who have obtained either the number of children they want in total, or the

3   See Chapter 1, the section 'Basic Characteristics of Those Interviewed'.

Table 3.1 *Proportion of respondents achieving preferred number of children at desired intervals**

	III2 %	III4+ %	V2 %	V4+ %
(a) All respondents				
Has more children than wants				
— Non-effective planner	10	60	17	53
Has fewer children than wants				
— Effective spacer	3	4	5	6
— Non-effective spacer	13	–	5	6
Has number of children wanted				
— Effective limiter and spacer	20	–	45	6
— Effective limiter, but not spacer	54	32	28	29
Inconsistent	–	4	–	–
Base for percentages	30	25	18	17
(b) Excluding the relatively sub-fecund				
Has more children than wants				
— Non-effective planner	17	60	23	53
Has fewer children than wants				
— Effective spacer	–	4	8	6
— Non-effective spacer	5	–	–	6
Has number of children wanted				
— Effective limiter and spacer	28	–	46	6
— Effective limiter, but not spacer	50	32	23	29
Inconsistent	–	4	–	–
Base for percentages	18	25	13	17

* The percentages used in Table 3.1 differ from those of Table 2.8 for the following reasons: (1) those pregnant at interview were classified in Table 3.1 as though a further live birth had taken place; (2) those who had alternative preferences (e.g. 'either two or three') were classified as having achieved the number of children they wanted if they had achieved either of these two alternatives.

number of children they want to date (although they either definitely or possibly want more at a later stage) are 80% in III2, 72% in V2, 35% in V4+ and 32% in III4+.

The following section examines how — by means of more efficient use of contraception[4] — those with two children have been more successful than those with four or more in limiting family size to the number of children desired and in spacing them as they wished. Related to efficient use of contraception are of course knowledge about such practices and attitudes towards them. These areas are examined in the final two sections of this chapter.

Use of Methods of Contraception
(1)   Before examining the types of contraceptive techniques used, it is useful to look at whether contraception has been used at all, and, if so, at what stage in the marriage it was first practised. Table 3.2 shows that all except one respondent have used some form of contraception. Other surveys show similarly high proportions of couples using contraception at some stage, although — as stated in the previous chapter — it is difficult to achieve accurate comparisons since other samples are drawn in different ways (e.g. they include people married for only a short period of time, or those in non-manual social classes). Peel for example stated that 'by the date of the second interview' (i.e. approximately five years after marriage) '290 couples (93% of the sample) had used some form of contraception at some time during marriage'.[5] Woolf found that 79% of the married fecund women in her sample acknowledged the present use of 'some method of voluntary limitation or regulation of their families', whilst a further 11% had used contraception in the past but were not at present using it.[6] In an earlier study in the United States, Whelpton et al. discovered that 'among white couples with the wife 18–39 years old, 81% had used contraception by 1960, and an additional 7% expected to begin use later. Of the remaining couples who expected not

---

4   The distinction between the terms 'birth control' and 'contraception' is often ambiguous. In this study 'contraception' will be used to refer to either appliances or practices used by individuals specifically to prevent conception. 'Birth control' is a wider term which would include, for example, termination of pregnancy and late age at marriage.

5   J. Peel (1972), 'The Hull Family Survey II. Family Planning in the First Five Years of Marriage', *Journal of Biosocial Science*, vol. 4, no. 3, pp. 333–46.

6   M. Woolf (1971), *Family Intentions*, Office of Population Censuses and Surveys, Social Survey Division (H.M.S.O., London).

Table 3.2 *Time by which some form of contraception had been practised*

	III2	III4+	V2	V4+	Effective limiters and spacers	Effective limiters, but not spacers	Others
	%	%	%	%	%	%	%
Before 1st delivery	43	8	33	12	42	29	14
After 1st delivery	86	44	72	35	63	74	51
After 2nd delivery	100	76	83	64	79	91	78
After 3rd delivery	–	92	94	70	90	94	89
After 4th delivery	–	96	–	88	–	100	95
After 5th delivery	–	100	–	94	–	–	100
After 6th delivery	–	–	–	100	95	–	–
Not at all	–	–	6	–	5	–	–
Base for percentages	30	25	18	17	19	34	37

to use contraception the majority (10% of all couples) were sub-fecund.'[7] The reason why the proportion of couples using contraception is even higher in the present study than in most others is almost certainly that the sample in this study excludes women married for less than ten years and those who have no children or only one child.

Table 3.2 also shows noticeable differences between the groups with regard to the stage at which contraception was first practised. Group III2 couples were most likely to start using contraception early in the family-building process (either before the first or before the second delivery). They were followed by group V2, then by III4+, and finally by V4+, only 35% of whom had practised contraception before the first or second deliveries. Again these results are in accord with the findings of other studies.[8]

When Table 3.2 is analysed by effectiveness of family-size limitation and spacing, the pattern is somewhat different from what might have been expected. Although those classified as effective 'limiters and spacers' are the most likely group to start using contraception before their first delivery (42%)

7   P.K. Whelpton, A.A. Campbell and J.E. Patterson (1966), *Fertility and Family Planning in the United States* (Princeton University Press).

8   See, for example, C.F. Westoff, R.G. Potter, P.C. Sagi and E.G. Mishler (1961), *Family Growth in Metropolitan America* (Princeton University Press); P.K. Whelpton, A.A. Campbell and J.E. Patterson (1966), op. cit.; J. Peel (1972), op. cit.

those classified as 'effective limiters but not spacers' are most likely to have used contraception at some stage before their second delivery. This pattern emerges because those classified as 'effective limiters and spacers' included both those who used contraception to space their children, and those who did not use contraception (at one or more of the intervals between their children) because they wished to have a child 'straight away'. The difference between group III2 and V2 in this respect (see Table 3.1) is largely due to this fact. Thus an examination of the pregnancy intervals of those in groups III2 and V2 who have the number of children they want shows that for group V2 41% of the pregnancy intervals[9] were periods in which no form of contraception was used and the respondent stated that she was pleased when she became pregnant. The equivalent proportion for group III2 was only 14%. In summary therefore it appears that group V2 respondents were more effective spacers of their children than group III2 because they were more likely to want to have their children 'close together'.

(2)   A second factor which may help to account for the greater success of those with two children in limiting their families to the number desired is that the methods of contraception which they used may have been of a more efficient type than those used by the groups with four or more children.

Table 3.3 shows the different types of contraceptive methods ever used, sub-divided by family size within social class. This shows that the most popular methods have been the sheath, pill and withdrawal (with sterilisation very common as a permanent solution by those with four or more children). These methods were also found by Peel to have been most popular among couples (interviewed 1970–1) who had been married for five years – 63% had used the sheath at some time, 51% the pill and 44% withdrawal.[10] Cartwright found a similar distribution – though with somewhat fewer pill users – in her study of the mothers and fathers of a random sample of babies; the interviews took place in 1967–8.[11] The differences between the four family-size-within-social-class groups are complex. In some ways group III4+ is much closer to the groups with two children than to V4+, i.e. they are less likely to have used withdrawal and more likely to have used the sheath and the pill than V4+. However, they are closer to V4+ than to the other two groups in their resort to sterilisation. Groups III2 and V2 are

9   Excluding the interval between the birth of the last child and the date of interview.

10   J. Peel (1972), op. cit.

11   A. Cartwright (1970), *Parents and Family Planning Services* (Routledge and Kegan Paul, London).

70

Table 3.3 *Methods of contraception used at some time since marriage*

	III2 %	III4+ %	V2 %	V4+ %
None	–	–	6	–
Withdrawal	33	28	44	53
Safe period	3	24	6	12
Chemicals alone	7	12	6	–
Diaphragm	3	12	6	12
Sheath	63	48	56	24
IUD	7	4	11	12
Pill	53	52	50	29
Sterilisation/hysterectomy/ vasectomy	13	60	17	59
Abstinence	7	–	6	6

similar except that V2 is more likely to have used withdrawal. Group V4+ is however the most distinct from the other groups, in having been most likely to use withdrawal and least likely to have used the more efficient methods such as the sheath and the pill (not including sterilisation).

(3)   One would expect the more efficient users of contraception to proceed from the use of the less reliable to the more reliable methods as they approached the family size they desired, since family-size *limitation* tends to be seen as a more essential concern than family-size *spacing*. Methods of contraception were therefore divided into four groups on the basis of the degree of their reliability in preventing conception.[12] In the first category (i.e. the least efficient) was withdrawal, the safe period and chemicals on their own; in the second was the sheath and the diaphragm plus spermicide; in the third the pill and the intra-uterine device; and in the fourth sterilisation. (Although sterilisation is undoubtedly the most reliable way of preventing conception one would not expect to see it employed by the most efficient users of contraception.) It can be clearly seen from Table 3.4 that group III2 has moved, at an earlier stage than other groups, from the use of no form of contraception to the use of some method, and then to the use of

12   For similar groupings see J. Lorraine (1970), *Sex and the Population Crisis* (Heinemann Medical Books, London); for contraceptive failure rates see, for example, J. Peel and M. Potts (1969), *Textbook of Contraceptive Practice* (Cambridge University Press).

Table 3.4 *Changes in contraceptive use during marriage**

	Before 1st delivery %	Before 2nd delivery %	Since last delivery %
(a) Group 1112			
Methods used			
— None	57	13	3
— Withdrawal, safe period, chemicals	14	23	17
— Sheath, diaphragm	30	43	30
— Pill, IUD	—	13	33
— Sterilisation	—	—	13
— Others	—	7	3
(b) Group V2			
Methods used			
— None	67	44	6
— Withdrawal, safe period, chemicals	11	22	28
— Sheath, diaphragm	22	22	—
— Pill, IUD	—	—	33
— Sterilisation	—	—	17
— Others	—	11	17

the more reliable methods. This group is followed by V2, then by III4+, and finally by group V4+, for whom the process of increasingly efficient contraception has been the most slow. For example, in the period before the second child was conceived, only 36% of III2 were using none or the least reliable forms of contraception while 56% were using the more reliable methods. The equivalent percentages were 66% and 22% in V2; 80% and 12% in III4+; and 95% and 5% in V4+. Thus although group III4+ appeared to have been as likely as those with two children to have used the more efficient methods of contraception *at some time* during their marriage (see Table 3.3), they differed from groups III2 and V2 and were closer to V4+ in the stage at which they started to use contraception and the stage at which they changed to the more efficient methods. For both group III4+ and V4+ the majority (60%) eventually reached a permanent solution to the problem of family-size limitation by being sterilised. (The question of sterilisation will be discussed

	Before 1st delivery %	Before 2nd delivery %	Before 3rd delivery %	Before 4th delivery %	Since last delivery %
(c) Group III4+					
Methods used					
— None	88	56	28	16	—
— Withdrawal, safe period, chemicals	8	24	32	40	12
— Sheath, diaphragm	—	12	20	24	12
— Pill, IUD	—	—	12	12	12
— Sterilisation	—	—	—	—	60
— Others	4	8	8	8	4
(d) Group V4+					
Methods used					
— None	88	65	47	47	6
— Withdrawal, safe period, chemicals	12	30	29	29	12
— Sheath, diaphragm	—	6	12	6	—
— Pill, IUD	—	—	6	12	18
— Sterilisation	—	—	—	—	59
— Others	—	—	6	6	6

* Where more than one contraceptive method was used in any of the periods of time specified above, the method last used at that time has been coded.

in greater detail in the section 'Attitudes towards Contraception', as will reasons given by respondents for selecting one method of contraception rather than another.)

Although it has been shown that the general pattern of contraception use is a move from the less reliable to the more reliable methods, there was also some shift in the opposite direction. The proportions reverting to less reliable methods were 20% in III2, 16% in III4+, 17% in V2, and 35% in V4+. In the great majority of cases this was due to fears about or dislike of the side-effects of the pill. (Again these attitudes will be discussed in greater detail in the section 'Attitudes towards Contraception'.) Once more group III4+ is closer to the groups with two children than to group V4+, whose use of contraception remains the least efficient.

(4) There is one further measure, however, on which group III4+ appears to be somewhat different from all the other groups. This is in the question of the number of different methods of contraception ever used (including sterilisation). Table 3.5 shows that whereas just under a quarter of groups III2, V2 and V4+ used three or more different methods, this percentage rose to 36% for group III4+. Group III2 was more likely than other groups to have used only one type of method.

Table 3.5 *Number of different methods of contraception ever used*

	III2 %	III4+ %	V2 %	V4+ %
None	—	—	6	—
One method	50	20	17	29
Two methods	27	44	56	47
Three or more methods	23	36	22	24
Mean number	1.8	2.4	2.0	2.0

This section on the use of contraception may be drawn to a conclusion by summarising briefly the differences between the four groups of respondents. Firstly, group III2 have tended to start using contraception early in their marriages, have quickly moved from the use of the less reliable to the more reliable methods, and having quickly found a satisfactory method they have thus used fewer different methods in total than other groups. Group III4+ are more likely to have started using contraception only after they have had two children, they have then used a variety of different methods — including the more reliable ones — but eventually are likely to have resorted to the permanent method of sterilisation. Group V2 respondents are similar to group III2 except that they did not begin using contraception quite so soon, are not quite so likely to have used the more reliable methods, and tend to have used slightly more methods. Finally group V4+ have been the least efficient in their use of birth control: they began using it at a later stage than others and are least likely to have used the more reliable methods. Like group III4+ they are likely eventually to have been sterilised.

The following examples of contraceptive usage in each of the groups will help to illustrate the type of behaviour patterns which occur:

III2. Two children, the first born 1 year and 5 months after marriage, and the second two years later

'We didn't think about it when we got married because we weren't worried when we had family. After the first baby we wanted to have a breather. We talked about birth control and my husband decided to use the sheath because there was nothing else for me to use. It was the only method we knew that seemed reasonably safe. We used it for a year and then gave it up to get pregnant. After the second baby came we talked about birth control again and I went to see my G.P. and she put me on the pill. She said I could have the cap or the pill and I chose the pill because I don't fancy the cap. I used it for about a year and then I read a book which talked about the side-effects and the danger of thrombosis. I got frightened, so we went back to using the sheath. We'll probably go on using it forever.'

V2. Two children, the first born 1 year and 4 months after marriage, and the second five years later

'We didn't mind if I got pregnant so we didn't bother about birth control when we got married. We agreed not to use anything. But after the first child we did talk about it because we didn't want any more children for a while because of money worries. I didn't mind about using something so long as he was willing to take the responsibility. He used the sheath – it's the one you hear most about. And I watched my dates – we didn't use the sheath when it was the safe period. Then after about four years we felt financially secure so we stopped trying to prevent pregnancy. Two children's enough so it went without saying that we'd use some sort of contraception after that. The methods we'd used before seemed quite satisfactory – they're the only ones we've ever thought of. So we've been using the sheath and the safe period carefully ever since.'

III4+. Four children, the first born five months after marriage, the second just over a year later, the third two and a half years after that, and the fourth eighteen months later

'We didn't use contraception before the first child. I just thought it couldn't happen to me. But we talked about it after the first child came. The doctor at the postnatal clinic mentioned it and advised me to go to the Family Planning Clinic, which I did, and was fitted for the cap. But I didn't like it so my husband decided to use the sheath because it was the only other method we knew. But we took chances, so I got pregnant again after about three months. After the second I still wanted to wait a while – it's best to get them out of the nappy stage before you have another. And the doctor at the postnatal clinic advised me to wait for three years because I was run down. So I went to my doctor and asked him for the pill. A friend of mine used it and thought it good, and I read about it, and that decided me. But after using it for nearly two years I got frightened and came off it – there were articles in the papers about it. I got pregnant straight away without having a chance to use another method. After the third child we went back to using the sheath – because I didn't like the pill or the cap. But my husband made a mistake one night so I fell again. I was very disappointed. I went to my doctor and told him I had to be sterilised – I was just utterly exhausted having children, I was at the end of my tether – I was desperate. It was a fight but I got them to sterilise me after the fourth child was born.'

V4+. Four children, the first born two months after marriage, the second three years later, the third eighteen months after that, and the fourth one year later

'Before we got married we never thought about it – I was green. Then after the first I was too frightened to take anything – I don't know what my husband thought. The District Nurse advised the cap but I didn't like the idea. So we didn't use anything again. After the second we didn't use anything either. We didn't like the idea of anything, and I thought I'd be lucky because I'd taken so long to fall with the second one that I thought it wouldn't happen again. Then after the third I was still feared to take anything, and we didn't have sex very often – but I think maybe I've fallen so easily just because we don't have sex very often. But when I fell with the fourth I went to my doctor and asked him if something could be done. He suggested sterilisation, and both my mother and my husband said it would be a good idea and not to be feared. It's a good thing it was done – I might have had another six kids.'

Knowledge of Contraception

(1) It is obvious that the use of contraception depends to some extent upon knowledge about the practice in general or individual methods in particular. It may be that one of the reasons why those with four or more children were less efficient users of contraception than those with only two children was that their knowledge was more limited. Other surveys have

found[13] – and the present study repeats the finding – that, when asked, the vast majority of women in all social classes can mention spontaneously at least one or two methods of contraception. However – as Rainwater has suggested – when women talk about their 'knowledge' of contraception they may be taking into account not only the purely intellectual dimension but also 'a social dimension (knowledge that a method exists that other people use routinely and effectively) or a psychological dimension (knowledge that the method one knows about it emotionally acceptable and within one's means to manipulate successfully)'.[14]

In this study relatively high proportions of respondents stated that before getting married they had known little about sex or contraception, and this was particularly true of those who now have the larger families. For example the proportions who said that they either did not know or only had some idea what sexual intercourse involved were 36% in III2, 33% in V2, 46% in III4+ and 53% in V4+. (Nearly all said they had known how a baby is born, since that had often formed part of a school curriculum, except apparently in group V4+ where almost half the respondents said that before marriage they had had no idea how a baby is born.)[15] Knowledge of how a woman can be prevented from getting pregnant also varied between groups (see Table 3.6). Those in group III2 were most likely to know either before they married, or early in marriage, how pregnancy can be avoided. They are followed by those in V2, with those in III4+ and V4+ most likely to know nothing until they got married or until they had had their first pregnancy.

(2) Although groups differ in the stage at which methods of contraception are learned, very little difference was observed between them in terms of the types of method known at the time before first delivery. Of those who knew any methods before their first delivery the majority said that they knew about the sheath (79%) and 35% that they knew about the diaphragm. Other methods were mentioned spontaneously by only very small proportions of respondents. By the time of interview, the vast majority of respondents felt that their knowledge had increased considerably. However at this stage there were differences in knowledge between those with two children and those

13 See, for example, L. Rainwater (1965), *Family Design: Marital Sexuality, Family Size and Contraception* (Aldine Publishing Co., Chicago); R. Hill, J.M. Stycos and K.W. Back (1959), *The Family and Population Control* (University of North Carolina Press).

14 L. Rainwater (1965), op. cit.

15 There were several stories of how the respondent had believed her baby would emerge from her abdomen.

Table 3.6 *Time when respondent said she knew ways in which a woman could be prevented from becoming pregnant*

	III2 %	III4+ %	V2 %	V4+ %
Before marriage	57	32	50	23
Before first pregnancy	77	68	72	59
Before second pregnancy	97	80	83	88
Before third pregnancy	100	88	94	94
Before fourth pregnancy		96	100	100
Before fifth pregnancy		100		

with four or more (though no clear-cut differences by social class). The results are given in Table 3.7, which shows that those with two children only are somewhat more likely to have mentioned spontaneously each of the contraceptive methods than those with four or more children. The only exception is withdrawal, which is slightly more likely to have been mentioned by those with four or more children. The most widely mentioned methods in both groups are the pill, the sheath and the diaphragm. Although those with only two children were somewhat more likely to mention all methods but one, and although they mentioned on average somewhat more methods than those with four or more children, it is worth recording that the vast majority of those with four or more children could mention at least one of the more reliable methods of contraception by the time of interview. These findings are similar to those of other surveys, although differences are found between studies requesting respondent's spontaneous recall and those in which recall is aided by the use of a list of contraceptive methods handed to the respondent.[16]

One further point is that the ability to mention a method of contraception tells one nothing about the extent of the knowledge of that method. Awareness may range from merely having heard the name of the method, to a knowledge of how to use it, where to obtain it, its relative reliability, etc. Unfortunately it was not possible to cover this aspect of the subject in the present study.

(3)   Another factor which may have an effect upon knowledge (as well as upon use and attitudes towards contraception) is the question of whether —

16   See, for example, A. Cartwright (1970), op. cit.; L. Rainwater (1965), op. cit.

Table 3.7 *Methods of contraception which respondent knew about at time of interview*

	Those with 2 children %	Those with 4 or more children %
Pill	92	85
Sheath	86	75
Diaphragm	75	65
IUD	46	38
Withdrawal	40	45
Chemicals alone	27	17
Safe period	27	15
Mean number of methods mentioned	4.3	3.6

and if so, at what stage in the marriage — husbands and wives talked about contraception. Rainwater, again, found differences between his 'upper-lower' and 'lower-lower' social classes in the extent of discussion and the time in marriage at which it was initiated.[17] It is in fact one of his central theses that 'the meagre resources of working-class husbands and wives for communication and co-operation with each other' is one of the major factors hindering the successful use of family-planning techniques.[18] In line with this, those with two children, in the present study, were said to have discussed contraception at an earlier stage in the family-building process than those with four or more, and the difference is particularly striking when comparing groups III2 and V4+ (see Table 3.8).

It is not surprising that only small proportions of couples were said by the respondents to have talked about contraception before the first pregnancy, since it has been shown (Table 3.2) that it was only in groups III2 and V2 that any form of contraception was practised at that time by substantial minorities. (It is interesting that more couples in V2 used birth control at that time than the number of respondents who said they had talked about using it. One respondent for example said, 'We never talked about birth control — I just told my husband I'd like to wait a while before falling and so he used withdrawal.' Another said, 'I didn't really think about it at all but my

17   L. Rainwater (1965), op. cit.
18   L. Rainwater (1960), *And the Poor Get Children* (Quadrangle Books, Chicago).

Table 3.8 *When respondent thought that she and her husband first talked about doing something to prevent pregnancy*

	III2 %	III4+ %	V2 %	V4+ %
At marriage	40	12	17	6
After first pregnancy	63	40	67	29
After second pregnancy	90	60	78	47
After third pregnancy	93	84	–	76
After fourth pregnancy	–	96	–	88
After fifth pregnancy	–	100	–	94
Never talked	7	–	22	6

husband decided to use withdrawal – I just left it up to him.')

Some examples of the range of types of discussion between husbands and wives are given below:

III2. Respondent wanted two children and achieved two.

> 'When we got married we discussed contraception and we both agreed that we wouldn't use anything because we didn't mind when I got pregnant. After the first, we talked about it again – we discussed all the different methods and decided which one would be the best for us. After the second child came we talked about it again and agreed to go on using the method we'd used before.'

III4+. Respondent has four children, but would have preferred two.

> 'Before the first child came we never talked about it – neither of us ever thought about it. After the first, I did mention it – I told him it was up to him, but he never bothered.' She said that when she was pregnant again 'we talked about it – I told him he should have prevented it, and he said I should have gone to the Family Planning Clinic. But after the second child we never discussed it – I still left it up to him, but he still wasn't bothered.' Later she added, 'After the third child came we talked about it again. He said, "Why don't you get the pill?" and I agreed.'

V2. Respondent wanted two children, and has achieved two.

> 'When we got married we both said we ought to use something to stop

me getting pregnant straight away, because we wanted to save up some money for the house first.' She said that after the first child came 'We didn't talk about it – I think he should have used something but he never did – he never discussed it. But after the second one came we did talk about contraception and he agreed to use Durex. But later I thought I'd rather be dead certain, so I told him I wanted to go on the pill. He just left that up to me.'

V4+. Respondent has four children, but would have preferred two or three.

It was not until after the second child came that she and her husband talked about contraception. Before that they 'never gave it a thought'. But after the second the respondent stated, 'I told him we'd have to be careful and he said that was a good idea. After the third child came we talked about it again – I said I was going to see about getting the pill, and he said, "Please yourself." ' After the fourth one she said, 'We talked about which method to use and we both agreed on the pill – he said it was the safest and cleanest and I quite agreed.'

Attitudes towards Contraception
Attitudes towards contraception are another important influence upon the use of such techniques. This section examines, first, attitudes in general and their changes over time, and then looks in more detail at the use of particular methods of controlling family size.

(1)   Although respondents can be distinguished on the basis of their attitudes towards contraception in general – i.e. whether they approved or disapproved, liked or disliked the idea of it, or ever thought about it – there came a time in their marriage when almost the entire sample were in favour of doing something to prevent pregnancy. The main differences between them after this stage had been reached were in relation to their attitudes towards particular methods of contraception, in terms of, for example, ease of use, method of obtaining, effect upon health, and so on.

Before the first pregnancy the majority of respondents stated that at that time they could not have expressed an attitude towards contraception: it was just something they never thought about at all or, if they did think about it, did not consider it relevant to their behaviour at the time. The reason for this was in most cases that they either positively wanted to have a child straight away or did not mind when the first child came, or that they knew nothing about contraception and therefore never considered it. It can be seen from Table 3.9 that by far the most important reason for neither using nor thinking about contraception was a desire for (or unconcern about) pregnancy. Over half of the whole sample gave that reason, followed by 20% who said they knew nothing about contraception at that time, and then by those who disliked or disapproved of it and by those who knew about it but 'just did not think' or thought they would 'be lucky'. This distribution is similar to that found in other studies (for example Westoff et al. and Whelpton et al.)[19] except that in such studies a slightly higher proportion gave desiring or not minding pregnancy as a reason, whereas fewer said that they had known

Table 3.9 *Attitudes towards the use of contraception*

	Before 1st pregnancy %	Before 2nd pregnancy %	Since last pregnancy %
Group III2			
In favour of using contraception	43	87	97
Desired or did not mind pregnancy straight away	34	13	3
Knew nothing about contraception	13	–	–
Knew but did not think of using/ thought would not get pregnant so soon	7	–	–
Disliked/disapproved of contraception	3	–	–
Other	–	–	–
Group V2			
In favour of using contraception	28	67	89
Desired or did not mind pregnancy straight away	39	28	–
Knew nothing about contraception	22	5	–
Knew but did not think of using/ thought would not get pregnant so soon	11	–	6
Disliked/disapproved of contraception	–	–	–
Other	–	–	6

19   C.F. Westoff, R.G. Potter, P.C. Sagi and E.G. Mishler (1961), op. cit.;
      P.K. Whelpton, A.A. Campbell and J.E. Patterson (1966), op. cit.

	Before 1st pregnancy %	Before 2nd pregnancy %	Before 3rd pregnancy %	Before 4th pregnancy %	Since last pregnancy %
Group III4+					
In favour of using contraception	8	48	76	88	100
Desired or did not mind pregnancy straight away	44	24	4	12	–
Knew nothing about contraception	12	8	8	–	–
Knew but did not think of using/ thought would not get pregnant so soon	16	12	12	–	–
Disliked/disapproved of contraception	20	8	–	–	–
Other	–	–	–	–	–
Group V4+					
In favour of using contraception	12	35	53	53	88
Desired or did not mind pregnancy straight away	47	41	30	6	–
Knew nothing about contraception	23	–	–	–	–
Knew but did not think of using/thought would not get pregnant so soon	6	12	6	29	–
Disliked/disapproved of contraception	12	12	12	12	6
Other	–	–	–	–	6

nothing about contraception. Whelpton et al. for example found that 72% of those who did not use contraception before their first pregnancy 'wanted children as soon as possible', 9% were ignorant of contraception, 4% did not think they would get pregnant so soon, and only 3% thought contraception wrong or too much trouble.

In this study those in social class V were most likely to know nothing about contraception before their first pregnancy, and those in group III4+

were most likely to disapprove of or dislike the idea of contraception.

It can be seen that those in favour of using contraception at that time were most likely to be found in group III2 (43%), next most likely in V2 (28%) and very unlikely to be found in groups III4+ and V4+. The great majority of wives thought their husbands had had similar feelings to themselves at that time. Again this is supported by the findings of Whelpton et al. who found that there was no significant difference between husbands and wives on the distribution of attitudes towards contraception.[20]

At this point in the marriage the overwhelming reason given for using birth control was in some sense financial: for example, 'We wanted to get a few things together', or 'We wanted to save up for the house', 'We wanted to get a bit of money together', or 'I wanted to get everything first — and paid for — and some money saved.' There were only four respondents among those who used birth control at this time who gave a different answer: one said they wanted time to enjoy themselves a little before settling down with children (III2), and three said they wanted time to adjust to marriage and to get used to living with one another (two in III2 and one is III4+).

Turning from the examination of attitudes to contraception before the first pregnancy to the change in attitudes during the ten years of marriage it can be seen (Table 3.9) that those in group III2 moved most rapidly to a position in which the vast majority of the group were in favour of using contraception. Reasons for not deciding to use contraception quickly disappeared although the desire for pregnancy remained longer than others. In group V2 a similar pattern can be observed although slightly more wanted to have their second child straight away or did not mind when the second child came. Those with four or more children took longer to decide in favour of contraception although those in group III4+ were likely to decide in favour of it at an earlier stage than those in group V4+.[21] Those in the latter group were more likely not to mind having their children straight away and so did not favour the use of contraception until quite late in their marriage. (These patterns are in line with the patterns of contraceptive usage outlined in an earlier section.)

The reasons for using contraception changed after the first child had been born. The most common reason, in all groups, in the interval after the first child had been born was to allow the first child to grow up a bit before the second child arrived: 'to give her time to grow out of nappies', 'to get him

20   P.K. Whelpton, A.A. Campbell and J.E. Patterson (1966), op. cit.

21   They did not necessarily take longer in time but only in terms of the number of birth intervals through which they had passed.

walking', 'to give him time to become a bit independent', and so on. For those with only two children, the main reason for using contraception after the second birth was that they wanted no more children. For those with four or more children, in the time after the second child was born, reasons were divided between 'allowing the second child to grow up a bit before having another' and not wishing to have any more children. After the third child had been born this latter reason — i.e. not wanting any more children — had assumed even greater importance, and was of course of overwhelming importance as a reason for the use of contraception after the last child had been born.

(2)   It has been stated above that although for the vast majority of respondents there came a time in marriage when they were in favour of using contraception, there were differences between the groups in their attitudes towards particular methods. This often made efficient use of contraception more difficult for some than for others. For example, among those with two children, after the last child was born 29% of those who favoured using contraception stated that at some time after the birth of the last child they had considered what they felt to be a more reliable method but had not used it or had ceased to use it after a short time because of dislike of some aspect of that method. For the remaining 71% there was no such problem: they decided which would be the most reliable method, or which would best suit them, and used it not necessarily without dislike — but at least resignedly. For those with attitude problems the method most widely stated as having been considered or tried was the pill.

Among those with four or more children however, after the birth of both the second and the third child just under half of those who favoured the use of contraception stated that they had had difficulties in accepting what they considered to be a more reliable method of contraception. In the interval after the second child was born most of the difficulties concerned the diaphragm, whereas in the following interval the majority of problems were over the pill.

For those who did not like the diaphragm the almost universal opinion was that they were embarrassed at having to go to a clinic and be examined, they did not like the idea of something being inserted into their bodies, and the thought of having to fit the diaphragm each time they had intercourse was unpleasant to them. (The Aberdonians' word to describe the diaphragm was that it was too 'scuttery'.)

Attitudes towards the pill are a clear example of the differences between the groups in the acceptability of more reliable methods of contraception. It was the method which received most spontaneous comment and was often discussed at great length. As an example it is therefore examined in more detail here than other methods.

Table 3.10 shows the different approaches towards the use of the pill. There is little difference between groups III2 and V2: about half of them had ever used the pill and a further quarter had considered using it but had not done so. At the time of interview 30% were still using the pill. Group III4+ respondents were similar to those with two children in the proportions who had ever used or considered using the pill but a far higher proportion had ceased to use it, so that by the time of interview only 8% were still pill-users. Group V4 were less likely than others to have ever used it, but a high proportion had considered it and decided against it. These findings support those of an earlier section in which it was shown that group III4+ was as likely to have used the more reliable methods of contraception as groups III2 and V2 but had used more methods all together, and that group V4+ was least likely to have used the more reliable methods.

Table 3.10 *Use of the pill*

	III2 %	III4+ %	V2 %	V4+ %
Ever used the pill	53	52	50	29
Now using the pill	30	8	28	12
Once used the pill	23	44	22	17
Thought about it but did not use	27	24	22	59
Did not think about it	20	24	28	12

Thus it cannot be assumed that when women know about the pill and how to obtain it they will use it (or will use it for more than a short period of time). Among those who once used it or thought of using it but did not, there are two major types of feeling about the method. The first is worry that they might experience adverse side-effects, or that they did in fact experience such side-effects when they tried it. For example,

> 'My doctor recommended it because he said it was the safest method. I thought it a good idea at the time. But after a few months I started to put on weight. I got really irritable and nervy. So my husband persuaded me to come off it for a rest. I felt so much better when I was off it that I decided not to go back on it.'

The second major feeling about the pill can be summed up as a general uncertainty or fear about what it might do to one's health. For example,

'I would have preferred the pill to other methods — It's easier and there's no mess. But I was scared — you hear about people dying from it, and I wouldn't know what it might do to me.'

Even those who are still using the pill are often unhappy about it. 'It's clean and certain but I still worry about it', said one, and another said, 'It's the lesser of three evils — sterilisation, another baby, or the pill. When I put it like that to my husband he had to agree.'

(3)   A further method of birth control which has not yet been discussed is induced abortion or termination of pregnancy. It is included here because although no one in the sample had had a pregnancy terminated since their marriage (nor did anyone admit to having successfully induced abortion), their consideration of the possibility of such action shows up an interesting difference between group III4+ and V4+ in the lengths to which they were prepared to go to limit their family size.

The groups with two children did not show that they had ever felt the need to have a pregnancy ended. They either had the number of children they wanted, or — if they had more — they accepted it on the whole with resignation. There was only one respondent who said that she had felt such distress at being pregnant for the second time that she had tried to induce an abortion (by the use of 'gin, mustard baths and pills'). This woman had returned to work after her first child started going to school, and the advent of a second child caused considerable disruption to her and to the family's way of living.

One would expect that the women with four or more children would have been more likely to have felt the need to end a pregnancy at some time than those with only two children. This is certainly true of those in social class III but not of those in social class V. Amongst those with four or more children in social class V, only one woman said that she had tried to end a pregnancy. When she was expecting her fourth child she went to her doctor and asked him if 'anything could be done'. Her doctor had apparently not mentioned termination, but had suggested that she might be sterilised after she had had the child. (One other woman in group V4+ said that her G.P. had actively encouraged termination at the time of both her sixth and seventh pregnancies, but at the first time she said she was 'feared of the operation', and the second time 'I was too far gone.')

In group III4+ however as many as seven respondents admitted to having tried either to induce abortion or to obtain a legal termination at some time. With five of them it was when they were expecting their fourth child, and with two when they were expecting their third.

One woman, for example, said that she had been 'really mad' when she found she was pregnant again. 'My husband was no help. He just said, "Oh you'll manage." But I was that wild — I tried taking mustard baths and jumping off the sink, but nothing did any good.'

Another said, 'I was in a terrible state. I tried to get a legal abortion, but the psychiatrist I had to see told me I'd better have the baby and then get sterilised. I took some pills to try and get rid of it, but it wasn't any use. I had to go through with it.'

This picture of a greater preparedness on the part of those in group III4+ than V4+ to take what they considered to be 'desperate' measures to control their family size may well be an indication of a more 'fatalistic' or 'passive' attitude among social class V women than among those in social class III. Such feelings will be discussed in more detail in the following chapter.[22] Such a difference between the two groups is also demonstrated in their behaviour with regard to sterilisation (i.e. whether it was a measure which was actively sought or more passively accepted).

(4)   The interest in the subject of sterilisation (as with that of abortion discussed above) falls not under the heading of the general question to be answered in this chapter, namely, 'Why are those with two children more efficient in controlling their family size than those with four or more?' It is included, rather, to answer the question of whether there are any differences between social class III and social class V in terms of their attitudes towards 'desperate' or 'final' solutions to the problems of controlling family size.

Sterilisation as a long-term solution to the problem of birth control was not discussed with all women, but the reasons for having the operation were discussed — as well as attitudes towards it — with those women who had been sterilised. They comprised 12% of those with two children and 60% of those with four or more. (These were a somewhat higher proportion than found by Thompson and Illsley but since their study was conducted approximately ten years earlier this is not surprising.)[23] Of those with two children, six had been sterilised — four of them had had the number of children they wanted, one had fewer and one had more than she wanted. In four cases it was advised strongly on medical grounds and in the other two cases the respondent herself requested it but there were medical grounds to support her petition. Only one woman now feels unhappy that it had to be

22   See also Chapter 1.
23   B. Thompson and R. Illsley (1969), 'Family Growth in Aberdeen', *Journal of Biosocial Science*, vol. 1, pp. 23–9.

done, because she wanted more children. This group is therefore not directly relevant in the present context.

Those with four or more children, however, were sterilised largely (though not entirely) because they were considered — by either medical personnel or by themselves — as having a sufficiently large number of children to make them possible candidates for sterilisation. Table 3.11 shows some of the most relevant details about the women who were sterilised. Those in group V4+ differ from those in III4+ in that sterilisation was less likely to have occurred as a result of a positive decision taken initially by the respondent, and there is now — partly perhaps as a result — less contentment with the fact of having been sterilised.

Table 3.11 *Profile of respondents who were sterilised*

	III4+	V4+
Number sterilised	15	10
Percentage of total	60%	59%
	No.	No.
Respondent took initiative	9	4
Doctor took initiative	4	5
Other	2	1
Respondent had		
— More children than she wanted	9	6
— Fewer children than she wanted	—	2
— The number she wanted	5	2
Inconsistent views	1	—
Respondent now		
— Glad she was sterilised	13	3
— Unhappy	2	3
— Has mixed feelings	—	4

There is therefore some indication that — as with abortion — those in group III4+ are more determined family-size limiters and less passive than group V4+ on the question of family-size control, after a certain number of children have been achieved. Two examples of the differing approaches to sterilisation are given.

The most extreme case in which sterilisation appears to have been imposed rather than positively sought by the respondent was that of a women in group V4+ who had had seven pregnancies. One was a still-birth, and in another case the child had died at the age of five months. When she was sterilised after the birth of the last child, the oldest of the five then living was six years of age. Two of the children attend a school for the mentally handicapped. After one of the children died, she said that she and her husband were advised not to have any more. The wife herself was ambivalent about the number of children she wanted. On the one hand she enjoyed having them – her husband was more considerate when she was pregnant and she enjoyed going into the hospital 'for a rest and some good food'. But on the other hand children brought responsibilities and money worries. Her husband, she said, 'would probably have just gone on having them – but it's not him that has the work'.

After the fourth living child was born she said she was told by her G.P. and a doctor at the hospital that 'I should go and get the coil because I wasn't fit to have more children. The Welfare told me that if I had any more I might have the children taken off me because I couldn't look after them properly.' However, even though she had an IUD fitted she became pregnant again. This time she said, 'They wanted to take her off me' (i.e. terminate the pregnancy) 'but I wouldn't agree. But I was told by everyone I had to be sterilised after I had her.' Her feelings now are: 'I didn't want more children, but I didn't want anything done, though in a way I'm glad because I've enough to look after, and now I may get a bit more freedom.'

At the other extreme was a woman in III4+ with four children each spaced one year apart. She said that both she and her husband had wanted only two or at the most three children, and wanted to space them about two years apart. The inability to achieve this goal was largely due to the respondent's fear of contraceptive appliances – 'the baby might be born deformed if you interfere with nature'. They tried using the safe period after the first child came. Then after the second she said, 'We never had a chance to use anything – I got pregnant again the first time we had sex.' After the third they tried the sheath – 'But it didn't work – they must have sold us duds.' The wife said she was very upset about that fourth pregnancy, 'but I was feared to use anything like a mustard bath or pills. I thought I'd better have him and then hope to get sterilised. I asked my doctor about termination but he said they were there to save lives, not prevent them. I asked if I could be sterilised after I'd had the baby, but they all tried to get me not to be sterilised. They weren't going to let me have it because I was only twenty-four. But they gave in eventually – I was determined to have something absolutely certain.'

(5) Most studies of contraceptive knowledge, use and attitudes devote a part of their time to a discussion of the influence of religion. In the present study this did not appear to be a factor of overriding importance, except that

there were more people who gave their religion as 'Roman Catholic' among those with four or more children than among those with only two. If the total sample size is considered as including both husbands and wives (i.e. a total of 180 persons rather than 90 couples) then amongst those with two children 4% gave their religion as Roman Catholic, compared with 13% of those with four or more children. Of these fifteen persons, eight were reported as never having been against the practice of contraception for religious reasons, a further five had once been against it but had changed their minds, and only two had remained in opposition to the practice. Two had never used any form of contraception, one had only ever used the safe period, and the remaining twelve had used other methods of contraception. Yet because those giving their religion as Roman Catholic are more likely to be found in the larger than the small families,[24] this is a factor which should be taken into account as one of the possible explanatory variables in the study of differential family size, even though Roman Catholics form only a minority of both groups and most of them do, at some stage in their marriage, use methods of contraception other than the safe period.

To summarise, it has been shown that those couples with two children were more efficient users of contraception than those with four or more. This behaviour is related to a variety of factors: those with two children were more likely to have knowledge about contraception at an early stage in the family-building process; they were more likely to know about the different methods of contraception; husbands and wives were more likely to have talked about the subject at an early stage; and they were more likely to favour the use of contraception when they had no children or only one child, and less likely either not to think about, be ignorant of, or dislike the idea of contraception. The greatest contrast was between those in social class III with two children and those in social class V with four or more. However, whereas group V2 was very similar to group III2, there were certain differences, as well as similarities, between groups III4+ and V4+. Those in social class III with four or more children used more methods of contraception than those in social class V with four or more, and were more likely to have tried the reliable methods. They were more likely to have attempted to get a pregnancy terminated or to induce an abortion, and also more likely to have initiated the request for sterilisation and to be content with the outcome of the operation. Group V4+ showed, on the whole, a greater passivity towards the idea of preventing an increase in their family size.

24   The difference was significant at the 5% level on a chi-squared test.

To end this chapter, illustrations of the two extremes of contraceptive efficiency are outlined in the behaviour of two couples.

The first couple is one living in a privately rented two-roomed flat. The husband had been a mechanical engineer but was now an ambulance driver because a slump in engineering a few years ago had made him redundant. When they got married they both thought they would like two children — a boy and a girl — because two children is all one can afford. They wanted to wait before having the first child until they had obtained and furnished a flat. They used the sheath regularly ('it would have been impractical not to use something') for two years and then stopped in order that the wife might get pregnant. Their first child — a girl — was born three and a half years after they got married. They wanted a second child when the first one became fairly independent. So they used the sheath again regularly for eighteen months and then gave it up in order to get pregnant. The second child — also a girl — was born two and a quarter years after the first. After that they both thought they would like another child, in order to try for a boy, but if it was another girl they would stop at three. The wife thinks they will achieve the number of children they want because they have been planned. They used the sheath again regularly for two years. They thought about the pill but were worried about the long-term effects so decided against it. When interviewed she was pregnant for the third time and was hoping it would be a boy.[25] She said she thought two or three children was the ideal number for people like themselves because 'it depends what you've got, what you'd like, and what you can afford'.

The other couple was very different. They had had eight live-born children (two of whom had died) and the wife was expecting another at the time of interview. They had had five homes since they married. The husband had had three unskilled occupations and had been unemployed several times. When they got married they did not talk about the number of children they wanted. The wife said, 'I suppose I thought two or three because that's what everybody usually thinks' and 'you can get on better with two or three'. They did not use contraception because they never thought about it and 'were not caring about it'. The first pregnancy was a pre-nuptial conception. After the first child the wife wanted to wait a while and then have just one more. She was going to get the pill but her doctor would not let her because she had 'bad kidneys'. He told her to go to the Family Planning Clinic but 'by the time I got to go it was always too late'. Her husband was in favour of contraception, but they did not use anything because she did not get the pill and

25 Since the time of interview the third child — a boy — has been born.

did not go to the Family Planning Clinic. When they had two children they thought that was enough, and the husband used withdrawal regularly to prevent another conception. But then the second child died, so they decided they wanted another one. After the third child they again used withdrawal but 'it didn't work out and I fell again'. By this time she said she 'was a bundle of nerves' with one child having died and another one being ill (he eventually died). They talked about contraception and wanted to use something but she did not like the idea of the cap. They used withdrawal again regularly, but again she got pregnant. After that she still felt that withdrawal was the only method available to them. They used it between each pregnancy. By the time she had had her sixth child she said, 'Once you've got over the shock of being pregnant it's all the same — once you have them, you want them.' She was going to be sterilised then but the operation was delayed for some reason and she then changed her mind — she was afraid of the operation. After the seventh and eighth children she was again advised to be sterilised. But she feared the operation. Although she believes that two or three children is the ideal number for people like themselves she also said it would make no difference to them if they had either two fewer or two more than they already have.

4
Cultural factors: values, norms, beliefs and goals

'Given the power of conventional society, members of the lower class are likely to be socialized in such a way that they recognise the normative status of conventional games even though they eventually discover that their own best bets, given the world as it is and as they see it, lie with substitute games.'[1]

Each of the four concepts which are here seen to be cultural – as opposed to situational – factors, can be involved in helping the individual to make sense of his social world and in guiding his behaviour. Values are those objects or conditions which the individual considers desirable; norms are the rules of the game – they define what one ought or ought not to do; beliefs are the ways the individual describes and explains how he sees his social world to be organised; goals are the objects or conditions towards which he aims or strives. Taking 'the large family' as an example, one may find an individual who thinks large families are desirable, feels that one ought to have a large number of children, is attempting to achieve this end herself, and believes, for example, that 'big families are happy families'. In this example each of the four concepts appear to be in harmony. This is however not necessarily the case. In the lower working class, for example, there may be individuals who have internalised some of the conventionally accepted norms but who may still have beliefs which are at variance with them, because of the fact that they see people like themselves as being unable to achieve conventionally prescribed behaviour. For example, in discussing family-size preferences we have seen women who think that one ought to have no more than two or three children but at the same time believe that large families are happier.[2]

---

1 Lee Rainwater (1968), 'The Problem of Lower Class Culture and Poverty War Strategy', in D.P. Moynihan (ed.), *On Understanding Poverty* (Basic Books Inc., New York).

2 See Chapter 2.

Empirical study of values, norms, beliefs and goals is beset with difficulties. They cannot be directly observed (though they may perhaps be inferred from observed conversation and behaviour), nor are valid answers easy to obtain in an interview situation.[3] To summarise briefly some of the major difficulties, it may firstly be impossible to formulate questions which do not elicit biased answers; the norms, etc. may be of a very complex nature which the respondent finds it impossible to verbalise; it may be felt that it is possible to examine only indicators of a norm, etc. rather than the norm itself, and yet the problem of ascertaining what is an indicator of what may be insurmountable; norms, etc. may not be consistent over different areas of social life so that if the researcher confines his attention to one area he may obtain an inaccurate assessment. Apart from such difficulties the interview situation itself may affect answers; for example the respondent may pay lip-service to what she considers to be the commonly held norm, whilst at the same time she may consider that norm inapplicable to herself and her life situation; alternatively norms, etc. may be genuinely altered — albeit temporarily — by the interview situation.

This study has not however taken the defeatist view that values, norms, etc. are impossible to examine in an interview situation. Quantitative analysis has been avoided, but it was believed that with careful analysis of respondents' answers to open-ended questions, their spontaneous comments, and other means of indirect assessment, a number of values, norms, etc. — concerning specific rather than general areas — could be elicited. We hope to show that these values, etc. may be used to promote — albeit tentatively — an understanding of wider orientations.

One further point should be borne in mind. As stated in the introductory chapter, this study concentrates more upon situational than upon cultural factors in attempting to explain differential family size. In the time available it was not possible to explore more than a very few aspects of those values etc. which are relevant to family-building behaviour. Each of the areas studied could comprise a separate research project, and it is to be hoped that further studies will add greatly to the data presented below.

Orientations of the Lower Working Class

Studies of the lower working class are noticeable for the proliferation of adjectives which they use to describe the condition of such groups (a glance at some of the passages quoted in Chapter 1 will confirm this). To list some

---

3   See, for example, A.V. Cicourel (1964), *Method and Measurement in Sociology* (Free Press, New York); Derek L. Phillips (1971), *Knowledge from What? Theories and Methods in Social Research* (Rand McNally and Co., Chicago).

of those adjectives more commonly used, the lower-working-class person has been described as passive, fatalistic, insecure, powerless, pessimistic, resigned, non-aspiring, resistant to change, present-time orientated; with feelings of marginality, helplessness, dependence, and inferiority; having a desire for present gratification, unable to control his own life situation, and unable to plan for the future.

From these and similar epithets one can distinguish four areas of social action, towards which the working class are seen to have orientations which differ from those of other strata, and in relation to which they may or may not have developed different values, norms, beliefs and goals from those of other social groups. These four areas are the future, the individual's control over his own life, the individual's influence upon wider events in his community or society, and material well-being and esteem. They are of course closely related, but as they are analytically distinct they can be treated separately.

(1)   The future. We hypothesise that lower-working-class groups tend to have a present rather than a future time orientation because for them the future is more uncertain and insecure than it is for other social groups. They are therefore likely to act in terms of present rather than future gratification, and to give little thought to the future. They may or may not develop appropriate values, norms, etc. as a means of adapting to this situation of uncertainty. If such a means of adaptation has occurred it is likely that individuals will place a positive value upon the present (for example 'better the devil you know than the devil you don't'), that they will feel that one should think of the present and 'take no thought for the morrow', that they will believe that the future is uncertain and cannot be foretold, and that their goals will be for present rather than future gratification. On the other hand they may retain the values, norms, beliefs and goals of the wider society (in which, for example, the future is more highly valued), whilst still feeling and being unable to act in accordance with such values.

(2)   The individual's control over his own life. We hypothesise that the lower working class are unable to control the major events of their own lives because they are socially and economically deprived, and their command over resources is minimal. Again they may or may not develop values, etc. in order to adapt to this situation. If they did so, they might for example value control by external forces; they might feel that the individual should 'take things as they come' and that others with greater powers of control should assist them; they might believe that the individual is not in control of his own destiny; and they might set as a goal the desire to find others to take care of

them. Again on the other hand they may maintain a positive evaluation of individual control, although it seems less likely that beliefs can be at variance with the reality of the situation than that individuals should *value* and *aspire to* that which is hard for them to achieve.

(3)   The individual's influence upon wider events. Because they lack power, those in the lower working class — either as individuals or as a group — are likely to have little influence upon the way their community or society is organised. This situation may or may not lead to a positive evaluation of their own powerlessness, a feeling that one should not attempt to intervene or participate in the way things are run (e.g. 'one should leave decisions to those with the know-how'), a belief that their position is one of powerlessness, and the goal of being left alone and not asked to participate.

(4)   Material well-being and esteem. The lower working class is the poorest section of society and at the lower end of the status hierarchy. Individuals may adapt to such a situation by negative evaluation of material wealth and esteem (for example, 'there are more important things in life than money'), feel that the individual should not attempt to improve his status or acquire material possessions, believe that the individual can do little to improve his position, and have negative aspirations for such improvement.

   This research project can only hope to provide some indication of whether or not values, norms, beliefs and aspirations in these areas have developed as a means of adapting to the economic, social and power situation of the lower working class. If they do exist, they are clearly of relevance to the expla-nation of differential family size (at least in three out of the four areas mentioned above). They would provide cultural support for orientations whose influence upon family-building behaviour has already been indicated. To recapitulate, if there is a present-time rather than a future orientation then the future benefits and disadvantages of having a certain number of children will not be taken into consideration nor will there be the capacity for forward planning necessary for efficient practice of contraception. If there is an orientation towards external rather than self control of life then the taking of active steps to prevent having children is unlikely to occur, and there may be a feeling that others (e.g. 'the state') will assist the family if, for example, they reach a position in which their needs outstrip their resources. If there is an orientation against the pursuit and attainment of higher material well-being and status, then the fact that a large number of children might inhibit such attainment is unlikely to be taken into account. The fourth area — that of the individual's influence upon wider events — is less directly relevant to family-building behaviour, though one might hypothesise that a lower-working-class orientation could affect the response of such groups to any concern about overpopulation. If, for example, governmental pressure was exerted to try to encourage married couples to limit their family size for the sake of the wider society, then the lower-working-class couple, who hold the view that the individual cannot influence wider events, might be less susceptible to such propaganda.

Two points should be stressed before the findings are presented. The first is — as has been mentioned in an earlier chapter — that the social class V group studied here is in a less 'unstable' or 'insecure' position[4] than others which could have been found, in that it does not include permanently broken marriages or one-parent families. Therefore any differences between the upper working class (social class III) and the lower working class (social class V) may be less distinct than if this aspect of instability had been incorporated into the study. However what this chapter aims to show is whether there appear to be any cultural differences between those with two children and those with four or more. Such analysis could only have been complicated by the necessity to take into account the additional variable of marital break-down or absence of a spouse. The second factor is that this study could only hope to explore a very small part of the individuals' orientations towards the four areas mentioned, in terms of their values, norms, beliefs and goals. What follows provides indications only, and not definitive statements.

The Future
Many writers have discussed and studied the orientation of the lower class towards the future. Cohen and Hodges, for example, found as one of the clearest outcomes of their study the preference of the lower-lower class for the 'familiar' as opposed to the unknown.[5] Schneiderman found among the poor 'an inclination to emphasise present time and present concerns over the requirements of either past or future, in contrast to the typical American concern for future planning'.[6] These writers are specifically concerned with the lower working class. Others however have seen a similar orientation for the whole of the working class, in comparison with that of the middle class. It may be assumed however that because the situation of the lower working

4 See J. Askham (1969), 'Delineation of the Lowest Social Class', *Journal of Biosocial Science*, vol. 1, pp. 327–35.

5 A.K. Cohen and H.M. Hodges (1963), 'Characteristics of the Lower Blue-Collar Class', *Social Problems*, vol. 10, no. 4, pp. 303–34.

6 L. Schneiderman (1964), 'Value Orientation Preferences of Chronic Relief Recipients', *Social Work*, vol. 9 (July), pp. 13–18.

class is even more insecure than that of the upper working class, they will have such an orientation to a greater extent. Hoggart sums up the position with regard to the future:

> 'There are many thrifty working class people today, as there have always been. But in general the immediate and present nature of working class life puts a premium on the taking of pleasures now and discourages planning for some future goal, or in the light of some ideal . . . Wage packets come in weekly and go out weekly, savings are traditionally for specific purposes, and a mistrust of saving is still quite common; you might get knocked down tomorrow.'[7]

Taking up first a specific point mentioned by Hoggart in the above quotation, we examined individuals' orientation towards saving. In terms of reported behaviour there were differences between the groups, particularly between groups III2 and V4+. Respondents were asked whether they were saving any money at present. Seven out of ten in III2 said they were saving, six out of ten in III4+, four out of ten in V2, and only two out of ten in V4+. Later, however, when asked what they would do if they had a little extra money coming in each week, most women in all groups said they would save it rather than spend it (i.e. seven out of ten in social class V and eight out of ten in social class III). Negative evaluation of saving was rarely expressed; only one person said, 'Why should you bother to save — you can't take it with you.' Most women were either already saving, or thought it would be a desirable thing to be able to do so. Those in social class V however (and especially those in group V4+) were pessimistic about their chances of being able to do so:

> 'In the position we're in there's no chance at all [of saving]. We need all we get just to keep going.'

But the desirability of saving was not denied:

> 'It would be nice to put a little past each week — for the little extra expenses that crop up — like birthdays or shoes wearing out.'

In this evaluative sense then there is some future orientation in all groups. The future of their children was another area examined, the hypothesis being that if there was a strong present-time orientation, the children's future education and occupations would not be considered. Women were asked whether they had given any thought to the sort of schooling they would like

---

7   R. Hoggart (1957), *The Uses of Literacy* (Chatto and Windus, London); see also Lee Rainwater (1960), *And the Poor Get Children* (Quadrangle Books, Chicago).

for their children and the sort of jobs they would like them to have. Table 4.1 shows that between seven out of ten and eight out of ten of all groups said they had thought about such matters (though not necessarily with regard to all their children; some for example said that they had thought about it for their older children but not for the younger ones).

Table 4.1 *Percentage of respondents saying they had thought about the kind of education/occupation they desired for their children*

	III2 %	III4+ %	V2 %	V4+ %
Thought about education	80	68	78	78
Thought about occupations	67	72	78	82

The type of education and occupation desired will be discussed in a later section but it may be mentioned here that women in group V4+ were much more pessimistic than others (as they were on the question of saving) about their children's chances of obtaining the desired education or occupation. When asked what they thought the chances were of their child or children obtaining the kind of education or occupation they would like them to have, social class III and group V2 women were divided fairly evenly into those who thought it was 'too early to say yet' and those who felt that their children stood a good chance. In group V4+ women were evenly divided into those who thought it too early to say and those who thought they did *not* stand a good chance; for example,

'I doubt it really – if they're anything like us.'
'God knows – it's all in the future.'

However even though they feel they cannot say what the future will bring, this does not deter women from thinking about it, and about what they would like it to bring.

A further aspect of the orientation towards the future is the hypothesis that the lower social class will have a preference for the familiar and a dislike of change. Indications of whether or not such an orientation existed were explored by asking respondents whether or not they felt they would be prepared to leave Aberdeen if their husbands were offered jobs elsewhere, first if they involved similar pay and prospects to their present jobs, then if they carried somewhat higher pay but similar prospects, and finally if the jobs involved both somewhat higher pay and better prospects. (Those whose husbands were, at the time of interview, unemployed were not asked this

100

question.) Groups III2 and V4+ appeared least resistant to change in this respect, with eight out of ten and seven out of ten respectively saying they would be willing to leave Aberdeen. Group V2 was most resistant, with only three out of ten willing to move. Group III4+ was equally divided between those who would and those who would not be willing to move. (Of those who said they would be willing to leave Aberdeen if their husbands were offered jobs elsewhere approximately half would go for higher pay, and half only if better prospects were also involved.) It is only possible to guess at the reasons for this pattern, but it may be that those in the most skilled jobs (i.e. group III2) feel that their skill is saleable in any market and would not feel insecure at changing their place of occupation, whilst those who are the least skilled and most insecure (group V4+) feel they have little to lose, and might even improve their position, by moving. (More will be said about job aspirations in a later section.) Thus although there is resistance to change among some women, it is not a predominantly lower-social-class phenomenon. Some examples of the kinds of answers which were given to these questions were:

> 'Oh yes I'd go, for a job with better pay — there's nothing to keep us here.' (V4+)
>
> 'He [husband] hates change — he doesn't like to push himself further. Now I'm a different sort of nature — I'd like us to better ourselves.' (III2)
>
> 'You're better to stay in Aberdeen. It's an awful responsibility moving. You can't come back and get a house again just like that with four children, if you don't like it.' (III4+)
>
> 'Money's not everything — we're quite happy here.' (V2)

Although only a few areas have been covered it does appear that, whatever their class position, women think about the future, do not consider it a subject which should be given no thought, and do not have goals purely for present gratification. They do vary however in the optimism or pessimism with which they regard their future.

The Individual's Control over His Own Life
Rainwater in discussing the poor says that they

> 'tend to have a basic belief that what happens in the world is determined mainly by external forces against which their own energies are not likely to be effective . . . Fundamentally such people are passive towards what they see as externally operating forces of fate and chance. They believe that what they themselves do is only part of an

overall pattern of life by which what actually happens is determined. One is not master of one's fate.'[8]

Klein compares such groups with a very different kind of working-class people:

'They were more in charge of their lives. They placed less reliance on luck or destiny. They felt more responsible for their own shortcomings and hence a little more on the defensive also. They expected more from life in general and from the institutions of society. They could complain to the local authority about their condition. They made demands; they were less likely to react with stoic acceptance.'[9]

Cohen and Hodges also found that one of the most consistent themes of the 'lower-lower class' was the belief that the individual could do little to control his life. 'You just have to live from day to day and hope the sun will shine tomorrow' was how they summed up this theme.[10]

Examples could be multiplied,[11] but what must be examined here is whether differences of this nature were found, in values, norms, beliefs and aspirations, between those in this sample with four or more children and those with only two.

The first question asked on this subject was one concerning the individual's ability to plan his life. Women were asked whether they tended to make plans or to 'take every day as it comes', or whether they felt they were somewhere in between. The results are shown in Table 4.2. Those with four or more children (especially those in social class V) were more likely than others to feel that they take every day as it comes. However the difference between the groups was not great, and half of those with only two children also tended to take things as they came. The replies indicated that such a response was due to beliefs about whether planning was *possible* rather than any normative reinforcement of taking things as they come. Only rarely did a woman state that she felt that one ought not to plan things. For example one

8   Lee Rainwater (1960), op. cit.

9   Josephine Klein (1965), *Samples from English Cultures*, vol. 1 (Routledge and Kegan Paul, London).

10   A.K. Cohen and H.M. Hodges (1963), op. cit.

11   See, for example, A.G. Neal and H.T. Groat (1970), 'Alienation Correlates of Catholic Fertility', *American Journal of Sociology*, vol. 76, no. 3, pp. 460–73; Brian Jackson (1968), *Working Class Community* (Routledge and Kegan Paul, London); Walter Miller (1958), 'Lower Class Culture as a Generating Milieu of Gang Delinquency', *Journal of Social Issues*, vol. 14, pp. 5–19; L. Schneiderman (1964), op. cit.; F. Zweig (1952), *The British Worker* (Gollancz, London).

Table 4.2 *Whether respondents felt they made plans or tended to take every day as it comes*

	III2 %	III4+ %	V2 %	V4+ %
Make plans	17	8	11	18
Make some plans but take other things as they come	33	28	33	12
Take every day as it comes	50	64	56	70

woman (in III2) said,

'I don't think you should plan – it doesn't pay to plan too far ahead.'

However the majority of women who took every day as it came did so on the basis of the belief that it was not *possible* to plan:

'We just live from day to day really. When we do make plans they never come off.' (III2)

'In the position we're in you can't make plans. You can only plan little things like a day out – and even that's a waste of time when you've got children – one of them could easily fall ill or something like that.' (V4+)

It does therefore appear that what we have hypothesised as a lower-class belief is fairly prevalent in all groups. Yet if one compares this stated belief with respondents' other statements about whether or not they have made definite plans for such things as husband's occupation, moving house, plans for children's education, what to buy for the house, and so on, then those with two children do appear to plan their lives to a greater extent than those with four or more. Nine out of ten respondents in group III2 and seven out of ten in V2 mentioned (at some point in the interviews) specific plans which they had made or were making, compared with six out of ten in III4+ and four out of ten in V4+. Thus all appear somewhat more likely to make plans than they felt was the case, and this was especially true of those with two children only.

Another difference between the groups was found (among those who felt that they did make plans) in whether the plans could be classified as major or long-term plans rather than short-term or relatively minor plans. Here however the difference was on class lines rather than on family-size lines. The plans of those in social class III were evenly divided between minor ones (buying things for the home, holidays or Christmas, clothes for the children) and the more major or long-term ones (such as buying their own house, moving house or job, insurance, the children's future), whereas two-thirds of the plans of those in social class V were for the more minor matters. This may be due to the greater income security of those in the skilled occupations, which makes relatively long-term financial plans more viable. Those in social class V were more likely to believe that one cannot plan far ahead. Some examples of the difference in approach to planning are:

> 'We like to plan for the future as much as you can – like when to have children, and what to buy for the house.' (III2)

> 'We plan for getting on and being more secure this year than we were last year.' (III4+)

> 'I make plans – planning week by week (not big things – you can't do that) but things like what to buy for the house, and when to have a night out.' (V4+)

Another question which was concerned with the individual's control over his own life occurred in discussion about the children and their future. Respondents were asked why it is that some children, when they leave school, get better jobs than others. It was assumed that among those who do not believe that the individual can control his own life, such factors as individual effort or drive would be stressed less frequently, and greater mention would be made of luck or factors beyond the individual's control, such as having had parents who could use their influence, or having been sent to a good school. Perhaps it is not surprising that the most commonly stated factor was seen to be 'brains' or 'ability', since this is probably the conventionally accepted reason for occupational advance (see Table 4.3). However, those in group III2 mentioned personality, drive or manner most frequently after 'brains', compared with group V4+ which put such factors in sixth place. Conversely group V4+ placed 'luck' in second place, whereas group III2 placed it seventh. These two factors may be taken as examples of individual attributes versus the influence of factors beyond the individual's control, and do show a difference between the upper working class (III2) and the lower working class (V4+). The other groups were in an intermediate position, placing neither 'luck' nor individual 'drive' in a low position.

Some examples of the kind of answers given to this question were:

> 'Some get better jobs because of their whole attitude – towards work and towards other people. Somebody who could speak out for himself would do better than a quiet person.' (III2)

> 'Some are quicker off the mark, and some are scared to push themselves to get a job.' (III4+)

Table 4.3 *Reasons* why some children, when they leave school, get better jobs than others (ranked in order of frequency of mention)*

	All respondents	III2	III4+	V2	V4+
Brains/ability/intelligence	1	1	1	1	1
Drive/personality/manner	2	2	1	3	6
Luck	3	7	3	2	2
Better education	4	4	5	3	3
Qualifications/certificates	5	3	3	9	3

* Only the five most frequently mentioned reasons are listed.

'There's just one reason – ability. If the whole world were built on ability it'd be a better world.' (V2)

'Oh – it's just a matter of luck. It's just a question of whether the jobs are available when you go for them.' (V4+)

Although there were indications here of a difference in beliefs, especially between groups III2 and V4+, when a question on a similar theme was posed, no such difference emerged. In this case the women were shown a list of attributes and were asked to say which of them they thought most and least important for someone to possess in order to get on in life. As Table 4.4 shows, there was a remarkable degree of consensus in their choice. In this question luck, cunning and the influence of rich parents were not seen as important, and the conventional wisdom of the importance of hard work and brains was predominant; in other words the individual is seen to control his own destiny and external factors are discredited. The reason for the difference between the answers to this question and the previous one can only be guessed. However it may well be that this question – being posed in a more general way and more removed from individual experience – tended to elicit the conventionally accepted answer: women were more likely to give what they thought was the expected answer. There was also some indication that women answered on the basis of what they would have liked to be the case, rather than what they believed to be the situation. For example, one woman said, 'Well, having rich parents isn't important – if we had money I wouldn't wany my children to feel we'd done it all for them.'

It was hypothesised that women who believed in the individual's control over his own life would be more likely than others to say that they were attempting to instill in their children attributes such as to work hard, to do their best, to stand up for themselves, and so on, whilst those with a lower-

Table 4.4 *Things thought most/least important for getting on in life (ranked in order of frequency of mention)*

	III2	III4+	V2	V4+
Most important				
— To work hard	1	1	1	1
— To be brainy	2	3	2	2
— To have been to a good school	3	2	3	2
— To be lucky	4	4	6	5
— To be cunning	5	5	4	5
— To have rich parents	6	5	4	4
Least important				
— To have rich parents	1	1	1	1
— To be cunning	2	2	2	2
— To be lucky	3	3	3	5
— To be brainy	4	4	4	2
— To have been to a good school	5	4	4	5
— To work hard	6	6	4	4

working-class orientation would be more likely to stress the more passive attributes of accepting what life brings, keeping out of trouble, and so on. Allison Davis, for example, states that the child in what he calls the under-privileged sector of the working class 'usually does not learn the ambition, the drive for high skills and for educational achievement' that those in other sectors learn.[12] Women were therefore asked to say what they thought were the most important things for them as parents to try and teach their children. This was an open-ended question and the answers therefore ranged over a very wide field. Most of the answers could not be fitted easily into the frame-work outlined above. For example the two most frequently mentioned factors were (a) that children should be taught to have good manners or to be well behaved (mentioned by three out of ten of groups III2 and V4+, four out of ten of III4+ and five out of ten of V2), and (b) that they should be taught to be honest and not tell lies (mentioned by four out of ten of III2, and three out of ten of all other groups). It may well be that the respondents were thinking more of the behaviour of their children as children rather than as potential adults and what would be most useful to them at a later stage of their lives. However some women did mention factors which were relevant to

12   Allison Davis (1946), 'The Motivation of the Underprivileged Worker', in
W.F. Whyte (ed.), *Industry and Society* (McGraw-Hill, New York).

the hypothesis considered here, and the expected difference between the groups appeared. Those in groups III2 and V2 were more likely to mention the importance of teaching factors which implied individual effort and initiative. Those who said that children should be taught to stand up for themselves, speak their mind, or pay attention at school, work hard, or do their best formed four in ten of group III2 and five in ten of V2, compared with only two in ten of III4+ and one in ten of V4+. Only one woman — and predictably she was in group V4+ — mentioned taking life as it comes:

> 'I'd like to teach them to take life as it comes — not to plan life for what it isn't — but enjoy life — be a realist.'

Another said,

> 'There's only two things to teach them: to keep their noses clean, and keep away from the U.A.B.'[13] (III4+)

An answer from the opposite end of the spectrum was:

> 'They should be taught to work hard. It's the only way to get on. And to have manners. To have a certain outlook on life, if you know what I mean — always to be on the look-out for a better job — it's the only way to get on.' (V2)

Those who lack control over their own lives will also be likely to stress, as the other side of the coin, the care or control which others exert on their behalf, for they will rely upon such care to a greater extent than other groups. They may believe that theirs is a situation in which such care is provided; it may be desired by them, and may also be normatively reinforced. However, if Miller is correct, then expressed wishes may be in contradiction to actual sentiments; he states that 'on the overt level there is a strong and frequently expressed resentment of the idea of external controls, restrictions on behaviour and unjust or coercive authority . . . Actual patterns of behaviour however reveal a marked discrepancy between expressed sentiment and what is covertly valued' — they often like being cared for and told what to do.[14] This area was investigated in this study by means of a series of questions about a variety of welfare benefits and other provisions of the welfare state, it being assumed that if those in the lower working class valued being cared for more than did others then they would express this feeling in

---

13   'U.A.B.' refers to the Unemployment Assistance Board, a term which went out of official use in 1940, when it became the National Assistance Board.

14   Walter Miller (1958), op. cit.

their attitudes towards the provision of various benefits.

Respondents were asked first whether they thought that the individual (or his parents) should pay for, or the state provide free of charge, school education, university education, school milk, medical prescriptions and hospital treatment.

The vast majority in all groups said they thought that school education and hospital treatment should be free for all people, two-thirds that school milk should be free of charge to all, and four out of ten that university education should be free. For medical prescriptions most people felt that the present system of payment with certain groups exempted was satisfactory, although 17% of those with two children and 33% of those with four or more thought that prescriptions should be free for all. The belief in payment did appear to be somewhat stronger in social class III than in social class V (particularly for those in social class III with only two children), but only in connection with university education and the provision of school milk (see Table 4.5). Some examples of the wide range of answers are given below:

> 'You should have to pay for some things. There are too many cadgers around.' (III2)

> 'You should help with your children's education – you can't expect to get everything for nothing – it's swindlers who are ruining our country.' (III2)

> 'The country needs people with brains, so the government should pay for them to go to university.' (III2)

> 'Let them pay for it [university education] – that's for the better class people.' (III4+)

> 'Those who've got more money should pay for things. Those who've got less should get them free.' (V2)

> 'They should pay [for university education]. Well that's for people with more money. There's a lot of people with more money – they should help those with less.' (V4+)

> 'Those who can't afford it should get things free.' (V4+)

Secondly, women were asked whether they felt that old age pensioners, widows, the unemployed, and women having babies should get more money, less, or about the same as they now get. Table 4.6 shows that the majority of all groups felt that old age pensioners and widows should get more, that maternity benefit should remain as it is, and that (except by those in group V4+) the unemployed should get less or that some of them should get less.

108

Table 4.5 *Proportion of respondents who felt that all people should pay at least a certain amount towards various benefits*

	III2 %	III4+ %	V2 %	V4+ %
School education	3	–	–	6
University education	20	24	11	12
School milk	27	8	11	–
Medical prescriptions	7	–	–	–
Hospital treatment	–	–	–	–

Table 4.6 *Proportion of respondents who thought various benefits should be increased, decreased, or remain as they are*

	III2 %	III4+ %	V2 %	V4+ %
Old age pensioners				
– More	74	90	81	88
– The same	18	10	13	–
– Less/some less/nothing	8	–	6	12
Widows				
– More	71	71	64	79
– The same	–	7	14	14
– Less/some less/nothing	29	22	22	7
The unemployed				
– More	4	–	–	12
– The same	14	21	39	47
– Less/some less/nothing	82	75	61	41
Women having babies (i.e. maternity benefit)				
– More	4	–	13	29
– The same	76	87	87	65
– Less/some less/nothing	20	13	–	6

(Only two people said they should get nothing but 'be forced to work'.)
However if one compares group III2 with V4+ there are indications of a more 'hard-line' attitude among the former group than among the latter. For example three out of ten of III2 think that widows, or some of them, should

109

get less compared with only one out of ten in V4+. Similarly eight out of ten in III2, but only four out of ten in V4+, think the unemployed or some of them should get less.

The common feeling about old age pensioners was that they did not get enough to live on, especially as prices kept going up, whilst the pension did not increase at the same time. One woman (in III4+) for example said, 'I've been speaking to people up and down the street and they say it's especially difficult for those who live on their own.' Another said, 'They ought to get their coal and rent paid for — they work all their lives and should be entitled to a bit of comfort.' Only rarely did someone say, 'It's up to them to put something by for their old age.' With regard to widows, again most people felt that it was a struggle for them, particularly if they had young children or for any other reason could not go out to work. A minority felt that if they were young enough widows should be required to go out to work. The most common feeling about the unemployed was that there were two types: one genuine and the other those who did not want to work. The latter group they felt should get less or be made to work. For example women said, 'Some should get less — that's what's wrong with this country — there's too many people who don't want to work' (III2); or 'If you want a job you can always get one of a sort' (V2); or 'My husband's never been idle but he gets the same as a man who's never worked' (V4+). Those who felt that the unemployed should not get less said such things as, 'We were better off on the *broo*[15] than when he was working — but we really needed it — it was hard to manage' (V4+). Such sentiments were usually expressed by people who had experienced living on unemployment benefit. Maternity benefit was rarely considered to be inadequate, though in group V4+ it was more common to find answers such as, 'It takes a good bit to keep a bairn — those with big families should get more', or even, 'Well, I've had a hard job to get mine — either my husband's wanted to spend it, or it's had to go on paying bills.' But in group III2 some women were hostile to the idea of maternity benefit; for example, 'No one's asking you to have children', or 'I don't think they should get anything — if you're going to have a family you should be able to afford them.'

To summarise, on the question of state care most people in all groups supported provision of benefits, especially to those with low incomes, although it was possible to detect a somewhat more widespread feeling that individuals should make their own provision and control their own lives in group III2 than in V4+ (with the other two groups in an intermediate position).

15   The '*broo*' stands for the unemployment 'bureau'.

In conclusion therefore there are differences — particularly between groups III2 and V4+ — in the extent to which women feel that the individual can or should control his own life. Yet the majority of all groups have what we have called a lower-working-class orientation on the question of 'planning' versus 'taking life as it comes' (although not when it comes to actual behaviour) and on the belief in external care (in the form of welfare state benefits). On the other hand there is a general belief that people 'get on in life' by individual effort or ability, and little support for the converse suggestion that environmental factors act as a deterrent or spur to achievement.

The Individual's Influence upon Wider Events

We have suggested that lower-working-class persons will participate less than others in events which are seen to have no direct influence upon their own lives, partly because they are more remote from the wider goals of the society and partly because they believe that such events are not influenced by what ordinary individuals do, but by more powerful forces beyond their control. Cohen and Hodges examine such feelings in relation to participation in voluntary associations.[16] They find very low participation in such organisations among the lower class and explain it in terms of (a) the inability of the lower-lower class to 'envisage events relatively remote from the immediate concrete situation, and a relationship between such events and one's own destiny', and (b) the fact that the lower-lower-class person 'does not feel that his influence within the organisation is great enough that his active participation would make any important difference in how things turn out'.

Amongst all groups of manual workers the level of participation in voluntary organisations is low[17] and the present sample was no exception. Respondents were asked whether they or their husbands belonged to any clubs or associations at various times (i.e. at the time after they got married but before they had their first child, at the time after they had their first child, and since their last child was born). Eight or nine out of ten in all groups said that they themselves did not belong to any clubs or associations at any of these times. Slightly more of the husbands were said to belong, but even among them six to eight out of ten did not do so. There was no clear distinction between the groups in this respect. The vast majority of those who

16   A.K. Cohen and H.M. Hodges (1963), op. cit.

17   See, for example, Murray Hausknecht (1964), 'The Blue-Collar Joiner', in A.B. Shostak and W. Gomberg, *Blue-Collar World* (Prentice-Hall, Englewood Cliffs, New Jersey); J.H. Goldthorpe, D. Lockwood, F. Bechhofer and J. Platt (1969), *The Affluent Worker in the Class Structure* (Cambridge University Press).

were members belonged to either sports or social clubs rather than to such things as work, political or church organisations.

Another type of behaviour which has some relevance for attitudes towards the individual's influence upon wider events is that of voting or non-voting in general elections. We hypothesise that those who do not believe that their participation makes any difference to how things are run will be less likely than others to vote. Respondents were therefore asked whether they had voted in the last general election. It was found that although most respondents said they had voted, there was some difference between those with two children and those with four or more, in that 87% of the former reported that they had voted, compared with 67% of the latter. However it may well be that those with the larger families found it more difficult to make time to go out and vote. There is also the possibility that there was some exaggeration of reported voting since that is likely to be considered the acceptable course of action.

This crude measure of voting or non-voting does not however tell us to what extent individuals consider their vote as instrumental in deciding the course of political events. One is here concerned with the concept of what is usually called political efficacy or competence, that is 'the feeling that some people have that their environment is a malleable one in that it can be changed in desired directions by acts of personal will and . . . that political "inputs" and "outputs" can be affected by the citizen'.[18] From the remarks of the respondents about their reasons for voting for one party rather than another it was clear that some had a greater sense of political efficacy than others. Many voted purely because they felt it was 'the thing to do', and preferred one party rather than another not because they felt that that party's policies were better or that their vote would help to put the party into power but solely because it was traditionally expected that they would vote for that party, and they had never considered voting for any other. Such respondents said, for example, 'It's in the family; all my family are Labour' or 'Labour's for the working class isn't it — we couldn't vote any other way.' Those with a greater sense of political efficacy made such comments as, 'Well, I thought they'd bring prices down' or 'They'll see that Scotland's voice is heard.' The former type of comment was more prevalent among those with four or more children and the latter among those with only two.

Another indicator of readiness to see the vote as having an influence, rather than purely as a traditionally expected act, was the readiness of

18   See, for example, G. Almond and S. Verba (1963), *The Civic Culture* (Princeton University Press); R.E. Dowse and J.A. Hughes (1972), *Political Sociology* (Wiley, London).

respondents to consider changing the party for which they voted from one election to another. They were asked whether they thought they would vote, and if so for which party they would vote, in the next general election. A comparison between their preferences in the last general election with that of the next showed that those with two children were more likely to be considering a change of party allegiance than those with four or more; 80% of those in III4+ and 60% of V4+ felt that their behaviour would be the same on both occasions (i.e. they would not vote at either election or would vote for the same party), compared with only 45% of those with two children. Some of their comments may help to clarify the distinction between those who did not consider their vote influential in determining the course of events, and those who saw it as instrumental. Amongst the former were such comments as:

> 'We always vote Labour – it's for the likes of us – the Conservatives are for the higher class.' (V4+)

> 'You can't choose between them.' (III4+)

> 'They're all the same – they all take off the working class.' (V4+)

> 'I just put down a cross – I don't know which is better. Prices keep going up whichever government you've got.' (V4+)

Amongst the latter however there was more often a comment on what was wrong with one party and how another might improve the situation:

> 'Labour's made a hash of it. I'm going to vote SNP next time – I think they'll put Scotland on its feet.' (V2)

> 'My father always swears by Labour – but I've found out how wrong he is. Prices keep going up. I won't vote that way again.' (III2)

The amount of interest which the respondent said she had in politics is also a possible indicator of the extent to which she *wants* to be involved in the wider events of the society as well as of her *belief* in the extent of the individual's influence upon such events. In groups III4+, V2 and V4+ only five women said they were fairly interested in politics; the rest said they had little or no interest. Only in group III2 did as many as a quarter say that they were fairly interested. (In all groups respondents saw their husbands as more interested in politics than they were: 50% in group III2 were seen as very or fairly interested, 48% in III4+, 44% in V2 and 24% in V4+.) Thus only in group III2 did one find a woman who said, 'Well, we're both fairly interested – we like to know what's going on'; whereas more typical were the women in group III4+ who said, 'I haven't time for politics' or 'I'm not interested – you just have to put up with whatever government you get.

113

Sometimes I understand politics, sometimes not. You just have to live with it and take things as they come.'

Although far too little evidence has been offered in this section to enable any generalisation about values, beliefs, etc. with regard to the individual's influence on 'the way things are run', such evidence as has been presented shows that no group participates to any extent in voluntary associations, nor do any have very much interest in politics. However the great majority say that they vote; and those with only two children appear to consider their vote as being of a more instrumental nature compared with the passive approach of those with four or more children. Further research would however be needed before this could be treated as anything more than a tentative indicator of the kind of orientation which is held concerning the individual's influence upon wider events.

Material Well-being and Status

This section concerns mainly the aspirations of the various groups for material or status improvement for themselves and/or their children. If they tend to have positive aspirations in this area then it is likely that they have a positive evaluation of such concerns and that they will be normatively reinforced.

Before turning to aspirations however, it may be useful to examine — as a background — the beliefs of the different groups about how this society is stratified, where on the social 'map' they would place themselves, and what sort of people belong to their social group.

Firstly respondents were asked whether they thought people could be divided into different social classes, and if so what sort of classes they thought there were in Britain today. Table 4.7 shows that those with four or more children were more likely than those with two children to see society as divided into two classes only, and as usual the differences were particularly clear in comparing V4+ with III2.

Table 4.7 *Respondents' estimation of the number of social classes there are in Britain*

	III2 %	III4+ %	V2 %	V4+ %
Two social classes	14	28	17	47
Three or more social classes	67	56	55	41
People are all the same	7	4	–	–
Other/don't know	13	12	28	12

Those who felt that there were only two classes tended to see the dichotomy as between 'them and us', 'the haves and the have nots' or 'the rich and the poor', whereas those who saw more than two classes saw finer gradations of wealth or status; for example,

> 'There's the really poor who have a struggle to make ends meet; then there's ordinary working people like us; above us there's managers and teachers and people like that who own their own homes; and above them there's the really rich — who don't have to work.' (III2)

When asked to place themselves on this social map (i.e. 'Which social class do you think you and your husband belong to?') those with four or more children were more likely to put themselves at the bottom of the scale than those with only two; and again the difference between III2 and V4+ was the most marked. Thus, out of those who saw two or more social classes, four out of ten in III2 placed themselves in the lowest class, five out of ten in V2, six out of ten in III4+, and as many as nine out of ten in V4+.

Finally, to provide further details of how the respondents saw their position, they were asked what sort of people they thought belonged to their social class. Table 4.8 shows that those in III2 were most likely to see themselves either as 'ordinary', 'ordinary working people' or 'those who are fairly well off'; those in III4+ and V2 were most likely to see themselves either as 'ordinary' or 'ordinary working people' (although women in III4+ were more likely than those in V2 to see themselves as 'poor'); and those in V4+ were most likely to see themselves as 'poor'. Some examples of the sort of comments which were made were:

> 'We're working class — those who are just managing to live comfortably and do without little.' (III2)

> 'We're ordinary people — all people are the same except titled people and millionaires.' (III2)

> 'We're normal working class — people who have to earn their wages to live but don't need help.' (III4+)

> 'We're working class — couples who are trying to make a living — they're probably both working, and they've got a house to keep up, and a couple of bairns.' (V2)

> 'Just people like myself, who manage — neither poor nor rich.' (V2)

> 'Those who struggle to make ends meet.' (V4+)

> 'We're the poor — those who have to put in overtime just to keep going — the rest don't have to sweat it out like we do.' (V4+)

Table 4.8 *Sort of people seen to belong to respondent's social class*

	III2 %	III4+ %	V2 %	V4+ %
Ordinary people/ordinary working people	37	52	50	30
Those who are fairly well off/ comfortably off	23	4	17	–
People who have to work for what they've got	13	4	11	12
Manual workers	13	8	–	–
The poor (i.e. those with low wages, less than others, have struggle to make ends meet)	–	24	12	60
People are all the same	7	4	–	–
Don't know	7	4	11	–

There are therefore differences between the groups in how they see their position in society, particularly between groups III2 and V4+. Group V4+ women are most likely to see society divided into two types of people, to see themselves in the lower class, and to think of themselves as poor, whereas group III2 women are most likely to place themselves in an intermediate position and see themselves as ordinary working people or those who are comfortably or fairly well off.

The question to be examined in this section is whether these differences in belief about position are reflected in differences in aspirations for material comfort or higher status. Do those in group V4+ say for example, 'We're satisfied with our position – money and well-paid jobs can't buy happiness', or do they have aspirations for the improvement of their position? Freedman et al. for example state that lower-status groups would like to be able to 'win for themselves and their children the higher standard of living to which they aspire along with other members of the population'.[19] Similarly Chilman states,

> 'Contrary to popular opinion very poor families are not resigned to poverty for themselves and their children. Particularly for their children they want the same things that other more fortunate parents

19   R. Freedman, G. Baumert and M. Bolte (1958–9), 'Expected Family Size and Family Size Values in West Germany', *Population Studies*, vol. 13, pp. 136–50.

want; a good education, good health, respectability, a secure and satisfying job, an attractive home, and a happy marriage.'[20]

Neither of these authors however cites any evidence to support his statements. Several questions were posed in the present study which may help to clarify the position. (It should however be mentioned that there are two problems in interpreting statements about aspirations; the first is the difficulty of distinguishing between goals which are real enough to guide behaviour and those which belong more to the realm of fantasy or daydream; the second is that of distinguishing between aspirations for an *improvement* in position and those whose aim is the maintenance of present position and a desire not to *fall behind* in status, financial position, and so on. It was not always possible to make these distinctions in the present study.)

Three types of issue were discussed, namely husband's occupation, material goods, and children's education and occupations.

As stated earlier in this chapter, if husbands were offered jobs elsewhere, out of every ten women, eight in III2 would be willing to leave Aberdeen, seven in V4+, five in III4+ and only three in V2. Most of those who would be willing to move would do so if income or promotion prospects or both were likely to be improved. However, it cannot be assumed that those who are willing to leave Aberdeen have higher job aspirations than those who would not be willing to move; other factors can of course be involved, such as a belief that the present job offers good promotion prospects, commitments to parents, desire not to move children from their present school, and so on.

To shed further light therefore on the question of occupational aspirations, respondents were asked how satisfied they felt with their husband's job, and how satisfied they felt their husbands were. Table 4.9 shows that, as well as being the group most unwilling to leave Aberdeen, V2 wives were the most likely to be satisfied with their husbands' present job. Group III4+ wives were the most likely to be dissatisfied, but overall women tended to like their husband's job either very or fairly well. They saw their husbands as even more satisfied than they themselves were, almost all of them being seen as liking their job either very or fairly well (those in group III2 being particularly likely to be seen as very satisfied).

The reasons of those who said that they or their husbands were not very or not at all satisfied were studied, to find out whether this was due to aspirations for higher pay or status. Such analysis showed that very few in any of the groups appeared to be concerned with such factors. Of the wives' own

20   C. Chilman (1968), 'Fertility and Poverty in the U.S.A.', *Journal of Marriage and the Family*, vol. 30, no. 2, pp. 207–27.

Table 4.9 *Satisfaction with husband's present job (excluding those unemployed)*

	III2 %	III4+ %	V2 %	V4+ No.*
Wife likes husband's job				
— Very well	37	32	35	(—)
— Fairly well/all right	47	32	65	(7)
— Not very well/not at all	16	36	—	(2)
Husband seen to like his job				
— Very well	60	48	47	(3)
— Fairly well/all right	23	44	47	(4)
— Not very well/not at all	17	8	6	(2)

* Percentages were not calculated because of the very small numbers involved.

reasons for dissatisfaction, six out of ten complained about their husbands being away from home too much or at inconvenient times (e.g. they were on a night shift or were long-distance lorry drivers), and only three in ten complained about pay or the security of the job. Similarly husbands' reasons for dissatisfaction were seen as pay or security in only three cases out of ten; others were seen as being dissatisfied with specific work conditions or with being away from home too often.

Women were also asked whether there was any other job they had thought of which they would rather their husbands had, or any which their husband would prefer. Table 4.10 shows that most respondents have no alternative preference, although such preferences are more likely in social class III than in social class V. Again the preferences of those who would like other jobs are not overwhelmingly for those carrying higher status or income. About half the preferences were for jobs involving more convenient working hours. The other half were for improvements in pay or status, such as 'a job in which he'd better himself', or 'a business of his own'. The numbers were too small however for any analysis by social class or family size to be worthwhile.

As a final means of assessing job aspirations, each woman was asked how she would feel if her husband were offered the chance to go on some sort of training course which would improve his qualifications or level of skill. She was also asked how she thought her husband would feel. It might be expected that such a question would invite an answer in favour of the husband going on the course. For what wife could say that she did not wish her

Table 4.10 *Whether other job preferred for husband (excluding those unemployed)*

	III2 %	III4+ %	V2 %	V4+ No.*
No other job preferred by either	63	52	82	(6)
Other job preferred by — both	17	16	–	(–)
— wife	7	20	6	(1)
— husband	10	12	12	(2)
Don't know	3	–	–	(–)

* Percentages were not calculated because of the very small numbers involved.

husband to improve his job prospects? However the question did discriminate between those with two children and those with four or more; whereas eight out of ten of the former thought it would be a good idea for their husbands to go on such courses (especially if 'it was going to better him'), only five out of ten of the latter thought it a good idea. Similarly, seven out of ten of groups III2 and V2 thought their husbands would definitely or probably want to go and only four out of ten of the others thought so. The main reason for their unwillingness was a feeling of satisfaction with the husband's present job (for example, 'He's getting on quite well where he is'). Another reason given was that wives would miss their husbands or that husbands would miss their families (for example, 'He did try once, but he came home after three days – He missed me and the kids'). Others said that they thought their husbands would not have the ability for such a course (for example, 'He hasn't got a head for that sort of thing').

In conclusion therefore, although it is impossible to give an overall assessment of job aspirations from the variety of questions asked, it does appear that on the whole the level of job aspirations (at least as far as the wives are concerned) is low in all groups, although marginally higher in groups III2 and V2 than in III4+ and V4+.

The second area investigated in this section was that of aspirations for material possessions. It has already been shown that those in social class III are more likely to be saving than those in social class V, and that those with two children are more likely to save than those with four or more. Most of the remainder would however like to save if they had the opportunity. An examination of the kind of things which respondents are, or would like to be, saving for will give some indications of their aspirations in this respect. Those with only two children were more likely than the others to say that they were

119

not saving for anything in particular, but were just 'putting some money past' or 'saving for a rainy day' (five in ten of III2, four in ten of V2, and three in ten of the other two groups). This may well indicate a greater lack of immediate or pressing needs on the part of those in III2 and V2. Of those who were saving (or would save) for specific things, those in group III2 were most likely to want what may be termed relatively major items of expenditure such as redecorating the house, the children's education, a new car, etc. whilst in the other three groups (and especially in V4+) the items of expenditure were of a more minor nature, such as 'for Christmas' or 'some new shoes for the children'. These findings are similar to those described earlier in connection with the sort of plans which women made (although there, those in group III4+ were closer to group III2 in being more likely than those in social class V to make plans for relatively long-term or major items).

Respondents were then asked to talk about the sort of things they would like to have but could not afford (if any). An attempt was made to get them to eliminate 'wild dreams' and discuss only items for which they felt a more conscious wish. As mentioned earlier, one would expect these wants to be of two different kinds; those which were aspirations to improve an already adequate material environment, and those which were aspirations to acquire needed items which could not be afforded because of a low income. Thus although those in group V4+ were more likely than all other groups to say that there were things which they wanted but could not at present afford (i.e. 100% of V4+, compared with three-quarters of III2, and two-thirds of III4+. and V2), this does not imply that they had higher material aspirations.

The kind of items wanted varied considerably, especially in comparing group III2 with V4+. In group III2 six out of ten women wanted either a house of their own or a larger or better council house; a quarter wanted a car or a better car; a quarter mentioned furniture or equipment for the house (for example, a new bedroom suite, carpet, refrigerator, washing-machine); and two in ten thought they would like a holiday. In group III4+ the three major items wanted were furniture or equipment for the house (four out of ten), a holiday (three out of ten) and a car or a better car (a quarter). Only a very small proportion mentioned housing. In group V2 a house and furniture or equipment were equally popular, being mentioned by four in ten of the respondents; only one person mentioned a holiday, and no one a car. In group V4+ − as in III4+ − furniture or equipment for the house was the most frequently mentioned want (mentioned by six out of ten); second in importance however was an item rarely mentioned by the other groups, namely clothes for the children or for the wife herself (four out of ten); a house or a car were mentioned by a quarter of respondents, but as with group V2 only one person mentioned a holiday.

120

Comparing group III2 with V4+ shows that the former are most likely to want to improve an already adequate material environment, whilst the latter are concerned with what are more usually felt to be the 'necessities' of life.

Expectations of eventually obtaining the things they wanted were relatively high in all groups, although there was a difference between those with two and those with four or more children. For example the proportion of all items which respondents felt they would definitely obtain or stood a good chance of obtaining, was eight out of ten among those with two children, and six out of ten among those with four or more children.

In studying each of the interviews with respondents it was clear that the vast majority of women had some aspirations for either themselves, their husbands or their homes. There was only a very small minority in all groups who appeared to have no great desire for a change in their present situation. For example, one woman in group III2, who said that she was the type who 'lives for today and lets tomorrow take care of itself', asserted that there was nothing she particularly wanted, that she was content with 'the way things are', and that she neither wanted to move house nor wished that her husband was in a different job. On the other hand there was another very small minority in all groups who appeared to have very high aspirations in a number of areas. For example, one woman in group V4+ said that what she really wanted for herself was 'a lot of new furniture, and a house of my own out in the country, away from everyone else — when the children are a bit older we might get it'. For her husband she said, 'What we'd like would be for him to get a yard and work on his own as a mechanic. His brother-in-law's offered to help him to get set up, but he won't accept help — he wants to do it all on his own.' The majority of respondents, however, fell somewhere between these two extremes.

The third area of enquiry was into aspirations for children's education or occupations. It has already been shown (in the section 'The Future') that over two-thirds of respondents had thought about the kind of education they would like for their children, and similarly two-thirds had thought about the kind of occupations which they would like them to have.

In the discussion on education women were asked to say what kind of secondary school they wanted their children to go to, and whether they wanted them to have any kind of further education before they started work. Of course, as all respondents had more than one child, a variety of aspirations could be expressed by each woman. However when women were coded according to the 'highest' type of educational aspiration which they mentioned (whether or not it was desired for all their children) there were marked differences between the groups, especially between III2 and V4+ (see Table 4.11). Types of education were placed in order according to their generally

Table 4.11 *Type of education desired for children (only highest aspiration coded)*

	III2 %	III4+ %	V2 %	V4+ %
Junior secondary school	23	24	22	59
Senior secondary/grammar school	13	32	39	12
Technical/commercial college etc.	10	4	–	–
University	33	8	16	5
Other answers	10	20	6	12
Don't know	10	12	17	12

accepted level of esteem (i.e. a non—grammar school education only in lowest place, and a university education in highest place). Group V4+ was much more likely than the other three groups to desire simply a junior secondary school education for their children,[21] and only one person had aspirations for a child to go to university. They said, for example,

> 'I think they've learned enough by the time they get to fifteen.'

> 'I want the kind of school they're going to get. The ordinary school up the road's all right — I don't think you should make too much fuss about education.'

Groups III4+ and V2 were again in an intermediate position; they were less likely than III2 to want their children to have further education after leaving school, but more likely than V4+ to want them to go to a senior secondary or grammar school. For example,

> 'I'd like them to have a good education — go to the grammar school and get their certificates so they'll get a good job when they leave school.'

Group III2 respondents were the most likely to want their children (or at least one of them) to have further education. For example,

21 Until recently there was a selection scheme for children between the ages of 11½ years and 12½ years. They then attended either Junior Secondary schools ('providing courses extending normally to three years, designed for pupils who intended to leave school at 15') or Senior Secondary schools ('providing courses of four, five or six years for pupils who intend to remain at school beyond 15'). See *Public Education in Scotland*, Scottish Education Department (H.M.S.O., Edinburgh).

122

'We want them to get as high as they can — university if they've got it in them. I think the oldest one will — he's got the right temperament.'

'I'd like the oldest one to go to grammar school and then on to the Nursing College. It's too early to say about the younger one yet — but I'd give them all the advantages I could — I don't want them to be like me — straight out of school and into work.'

On the question of the kind of jobs desired for the children there was a remarkable degree of consensus throughout all groups; almost all respondents wanted their sons to have a trade or a skilled-manual job, or said 'not a dead-end job but something with a bit of training'. Groups III4+ and V4+ were no less likely than the other two groups to give such answers. Two out of ten in groups III2, III4+ and V2 mentioned non-manual occupations of some kind, but none in group V4+. No one mentioned unskilled occupations. There was a similar degree of consensus over girls' jobs; almost all respondents wanted their daughters to be either shop assistants, hairdressers, nurses, or secretaries or typists. Only one respondent mentioned unskilled work; and there was a minority in all groups who thought that it did not matter what kind of jobs girls obtained (e.g. 'They're only going to get married — so it doesn't matter what they do'). Examples of the kind of answers received are:

'I'd like them to have something with a career — so they could have a better life than us — doctors or teachers or things like that.' (III2)

'I'd like the boys to have a trade, and the girl to go in for office work, or nursing, but we don't know what they're going to be good at yet.' (III4+)

'I'd like the boy to have a skilled job, but it doesn't matter for girls — they marry young nowadays.' (V2)

'It would be nice for the girls to go in for nursing or hairdressing, and the boys to be mechanics or joiners, but it really depends on themselves, and what they want to do.' (V4+)

The main difference between the groups — as has been indicated in an earlier section — was in the degree of optimism or pessimism which they felt about the likelihood of the children achieving the desired occupation. Group V4+ was more likely than all other groups to feel doubtful that their children would get the skilled occupations which on the whole they desired for them.

To conclude this section, it appears that on the whole the similarities between the groups are more noticeable than the differences. Aspirations with regard to husband's occupation are relatively low in all groups: all respondents tend to be reasonably content with their husbands' present job, see their husbands as relatively satisfied, and have no definite preferences for alternative occupations. Even where there is dissatisfaction it is not generally due to questions of pay or occupational status but to more specific work conditions. Secondly almost all respondents feel that there are certain material possessions which they would like but cannot at present afford, and most people are optimistic about their chances of eventually obtaining such things. Finally there is a high level of agreement about the kinds of occupations respondents would like for their children if they could choose.

The differences which have been observed mainly concern the *type* of material possessions to which the women aspire. They are particularly marked in comparing group III2 with V4+ (with the other two groups in an intermediate position). Group III2 is for example more likely than other groups to be saving for relatively major items, and to want expensive things such as a house of their own. Group V4+ on the other hand is most likely to want to save for items of a relatively minor nature, and to desire what others might consider the more essential requisites of clothes or furniture. Unlike III2 they also tended not to aspire beyond junior secondary education for their children, although in common with the others they did want to see their children in skilled occupations on leaving school.

Differences between the Groups in Values, Norms, Beliefs and Goals
This chapter has attempted to discover whether there is a marked difference between those with four or more children and those with only two, in certain of their values, norms, beliefs and goals. If such a difference existed one might then be able to conclude that such cultural factors provide an important or even a sufficient explanation of the differences in family size. We have chosen those four areas of social action which were considered most relevant to family-building behaviour, and which are most commonly stated as showing differences between the lower working class and other working-class groups. Whilst we could not hope to cover each of these areas adequately, it was hoped that sufficient indications could be provided to show whether or not there were any major and consistent differences between the four groups studied.

Although a great deal of information has been reported, showing both similarities and differences between the groups, it is possible to draw together the major findings of this chapter in order to go some way towards answering the question of whether it is in their culture rather than their situation that those with four or more children differ from those with only two.

Firstly we would suggest that, to the extent that there is some evidence of a lower-class culture, it is most marked — as might be expected — amongst those in social class V with four or more children, and less so among those in social class III with four or more children. Group III4+ may be more similar to group V4+ in certain respects than are the other two groups, but the difference between III4+ and those with two children is often not over-whelming. (For example III4+ have somewhat higher educational aspirations for their children than V4+, they are somewhat less likely to believe that one must 'take every day as it comes', and they are somewhat less likely to believe that they belong to the lowest social class.) It was frequently found that, where there were differences between the groups, those in III4+ and V2 were in a similar intermediate position between the extremes of the other two groups.

However, it should not be concluded that there is strong evidence of the existence of lower-class culture amongst those in group V4+. On the contrary, it appears reasonable to conclude that the groups were more remarkable for their cultural similarities than their differences. With regard to values, there was little negative evaluation of the future, nor of the desirability of improving one's material and status position. Normatively, few thought that one should not think of the future, most felt that the individual should not be left without the support and aid of outside bodies (but tended to believe in state provision), and few felt that one should not seek improved wealth and status. As for what the respondents actually desired or were trying to achieve, most wanted little to do with the way their society was governed, nor did they show a high degree of interest in improving their husbands' occupational position, but most of them wanted a better standard of living (in the shape of housing, furnishings and the other marks of the affluent society) and wanted skilled and secure jobs for their children. On the question of beliefs, however, there was less consensus, although even here there was wide agreement over the belief that the individual could not plan his life, and that people get on in life by having brains and working hard and not by coming from a wealthy home background.

The area in which differences between the groups was most evident was — as has been indicated — that of beliefs. There were few notable differences in any other area. As stated earlier in this chapter, if sectors of society differ situationally from one another this does not necessarily prevent them from valuing or aspiring to similar behaviour, nor from having similar norms about how people should behave, but it is likely to prevent them from having similar beliefs about what kind of behaviour is and is not possible for the individual. Thus those in group V4+ were more pessimistic than others about the possibility of looking towards the future, about the possibility of individuals planning their lives or 'getting on' in life through individual effort; they appeared somewhat less likely to believe in the individual's influence upon wider events; and they were more pessimistic than others about the

125

chances of their children achieving the kind of jobs which they would like for them.

Differences in areas other than that of beliefs were also closely associated with situational factors. In relation to norms, group V4+ only differed substantially from others over the question of support for higher unemployment benefit — a subject on which they were more likely than all other groups to have had personal experience (see the following chapter). They were also somewhat more likely than others to think that other types of welfare state provision should be free or benefits increased. On the subject of wants or aspirations they tended to be less ambitious than other groups, a tendency which was probably influenced by their low level of income and by their beliefs about the possibility of achieving such ends.

This chapter therefore indicates that it is the situation of those in the lower working class which may have a greater influence upon their orientations and thus upon their actual behaviour, than their values, goals and norms. Beliefs however do appear to be affected by situational factors, and the following chapter will therefore explore the extent of the difference between the groups with regard to such factors.

5
Situational factors and patterns of behaviour

'The way of life associated with low-skilled manual labour
involves a characteristic set of life conditions and customary
behavioural practices.'[1]

The previous chapter has indicated that in terms of certain values, norms and
goals there is a high level of similarity between those with two children and
those with four or more, both in social class III and in social class V. It was
only in relation to beliefs that − in the four areas of orientation studied − a
clear difference was found between those in social class V with four or more
children, and all other groups. In other words, in the areas studied no strong
cultural differences between the groups were discovered which could substantially account for differences in family-building behaviour. However, as
has been suggested in Chapter 1, even though the values, norms and goals of
lower-working-class people may not appear to differ from those of other
strata, they are likely to develop distinct orientations towards certain spheres
of action (as a result of recognising or adapting to their situation of
deprivation and insecurity). These orientations will result in certain distinct
patterns of behaviour, which may not be normatively reinforced but which
may be seen by the actors as the only possible ways of acting, given their
circumstances. In other words behaviour itself indicates a particular type of
orientation, even though the way individuals feel they would like to behave,
and the way they feel people should behave, may not be in accordance with
the way they themselves act. For example, a lower-working-class person is
likely to have a 'present-time' orientation because of the uncertainty of his
future. Because he knows he cannot plan for his future he behaves in terms of
present rather than future gratification. When asked, however, he may nonetheless feel that in general people should look to the future, and would like to

1   Walter Miller (1968), 'The Elimination of the American Lower Class as National
     Policy: A Critique of the Ideology of the Poverty Movement of the 1960s', in
     D.P. Moynihan (ed.), *On Understanding Poverty* (Basic Books Inc., New York).

do so himself.[2] The position which is adopted in this study may be clarified by comparing it with Rodman's concept of the 'lower-class value stretch'.[3] Rodman believes that lower-class groups will support the values of other strata, but suggests that they may also develop values specific to their group, as a means of adapting to their existential situation. This may indeed occur, but what may also happen is that rather than develop alternative values or norms, lower-class people may merely recognise their own inability to behave in certain ways and thus develop typical ways of acting, or orientations, which do not appear to be normatively reinforced. For example, if one assumes that — with regard to the question of family size — the middle-class family-size norm is two or three children, then a lower-class person with more than three children may either assert

(1)   that she disapproves of the middle-class norm, and thinks people ought to have four or more children, or

(2)   that two or three children is the right number for some but that people like herself should have four or more, or

(3)   that she knows she has more children than one ought to have but feels that she had no choice in the matter and that she just had to accept the number of children she got.

Some may argue that, if this is the case, then the researcher should attempt to investigate directly whether the respondent feels unable to achieve what she would like to achieve, rather than attempt to infer orientations from behaviour. To some extent this method can be adopted, yet it may be that in an interview situation the respondent is led to give answers in accordance with what she feels to be the accepted values and norms (and perhaps values and norms to which she also adheres) rather than to consider specifically the reality of her own situation. A second difficulty is that the types of orientation with which we are concerned are difficult to formulate as questions, even when related to a specific area of action. For example, one may hypothesise that the reasons for marrying at a particular time indicate either a future or a present-time orientation towards the event of marriage, and either the individuals' sense of planning their lives or of being precipitated into action by external factors (for example, marriage can take place at a time when the couple have planned their future accommodation, made financial arrangements, and so on, or it can occur relatively soon after the decision to marry

2   See Lee Rainwater (1968), 'The Problem of Lower Class Culture and Poverty War Strategy', in D.P. Moynihan (ed.), op. cit.

3   Hyman Rodman (1963), 'The Lower-Class Value Stretch', *Social Forces*, vol. 42, no. 2 (December), pp. 205–15.

has been made, and when little thought or planning of future arrangements has taken place). It would be difficult to formulate questions to assess adequately whether a respondent felt that, for people like her, marriage was an event for which one could plan and think ahead. It may be that relatively precipitate marriage is merely one of the typical ways of acting for lower-class groups, and that they would find it difficult to formulate reasons for why this is so. (For some people however a norm regarding precipitate marriage may exist, and where this is the case respondents can answer in terms of such a norm, such as, for example, 'I don't believe in long engagements.') In most cases however it was felt that behaviour itself would provide more useful insights into types of orientation than an attempt to obtain respondents' own formulations of their orientations.

A variety of areas of behaviour will be examined in this chapter, and it is hoped that — by attempting to discover whether in other areas of behaviour there are indications of differing orientations between the four groups studied — further support will be added to the hypothesis that it is differing types of orientation that help to account for differential family-building behaviour.

We have suggested that differing types of orientation towards areas of social action arise as a means of adaptation to a particular social and economic situation. What we have called lower-working-class orientations result from a situation of relative social and economic deprivation and in-security. The first task of this chapter therefore is to examine whether or not the lower-working-class groups do differ situationally from the upper-working-class groups. However, not all lower-working-class couples have large families, neither do all those in the upper working class have small families. The reason for this may be that they have developed different orientations as a result of differing experience of deprivation and insecurity. On the other hand quite separate factors may be in operation to account for their family-building behaviour. It is therefore necessary to examine the patterns of deprivation and insecurity experienced by each of the four groups of respondents studied.

Before turning to the examination of situational factors one further point should be mentioned. Although one can distinguish theoretically between situations of deprivation, etc. and behaviour arising out of the possession of certain types of orientation, such a distinction is in practice not in all cases easy to make. For example, for a husband to become unemployed may be treated as a situation of deprivation for the man and his family since it is likely to involve loss of income and the insecurity of not knowing when he will obtain another job. On the other hand unemployment may occur as a result of a certain type of orientation towards work. (For example, if a person does not believe that the individual can control his own life, and if he believes that external agencies will care for him if he is unemployed then he may not make an effort to retain a job.) In the discussion which follows therefore we have attempted to take as examples of behaviour resulting from particular types of orientation only those actions which do not necessarily imply, or result from, deprivation or insecurity. (For example, to be in a low-skilled occupation is to be deprived, whereas to be pregnant at marriage is not *necessarily* to be deprived but may be an indicator of a particular type of orientation towards marriage and family-building.)

The Situation of the Lower Working Class
For the thesis of this study to be upheld it is necessary to hypothesise that (1) those in social class V with four or more children have been more deprived than those in the same social class with only two children (unless of course there is a separate reason, such as sub-fecundity, to account for the small family in social class V), and (2) those in social class III with four or more children have been more deprived than those in the same class with only two children (again unless there is a different explanation for the large family in social class III, such as strong religious beliefs prohibiting the use of contraception).

The situation of the lower working class has been summarily referred to as one of deprivation and insecurity. The crux of this situation is that of the occupational position of such people, i.e. the fact that they can obtain only low-skilled or unskilled occupations. The other characteristics of their situation are either factors which lead to the possession of low-skilled jobs or result from such occupations. Walter Miller has summed up the job situation of the lower class as

> 'a pattern of work involvement entailing predominantly non-specialised physical labour at low-skilled levels and incorporating varying degrees of recurrent intermittency as demands for low-skilled labour of different kinds wax and wane with changes in the seasons and/or the supply-and-demand circumstances of the market'.[4]

As Miller suggests, such occupations are likely to involve the insecurity of intermittent unemployment or falls in income. With these there also goes 'a level of monetary and/or non-monetary recompense generally commensurate with low levels of occupational skill, based on a societal reward system that grants higher levels of reward to those whose occupations involve higher levels

4   Walter Miller (1968), op. cit.

of skill and responsibility'.[5] Thirdly such occupations place individuals in a powerless position in that (1) their bargaining power is weak since they are easily replaceable, and (2) they have less opportunity than other workers for autonomous decision-taking in their work. Fourthly the possession of low-skilled occupations brings low status, and probably also a feeling of deprivation. As well as the above factors which are consequent upon the possession of a low-skilled occupation, there are other situational character-istics which are generally seen to lead to such an occupational position; these are a family background of deprivation and insecurity which is likely to contribute to a low standard of physical well-being and a relatively low potential for educational and occupational achievement, physical disability or ill-health, and a low standard of education.

The situational factors which have been mentioned are closely inter-connected, so that any one of the effects of low-skilled occupation can in turn become a cause of further deprivation. Similarly one of the causes can become an effect either for the individual himself or for his children (for example, hard physical labour can result in illness or disability as well as being a cause of a low-skilled job; a father in a low-skilled occupation is likely to live in an area in which there may be a low standard of school facilities, and thus his children suffer from educational deprivation). However it is of course possible to break out of the circle of deprivation: a child may be able to make good educational progress, a man may be able to obtain stable employment and avoid unemployment, and so on. (This may mean — as will be argued later — that lower-working-class orientations either do not develop or are weakened or abandoned.)

In this section therefore will be examined those situational factors which make up the position of deprivation and insecurity of the lower working class. They can be divided into three sections:

(1) background factors affecting the respondent and her husband (whether their fathers were in low-skilled occupations, unemployed or not present when they were children; the number of siblings of the wife and husband; whether or not the wife or husband had any further education or training after leaving school);

(2) occupational experience (wife's occupation before marriage; husband's occupation since marriage; and occupational mobility);

(3) consequent factors (whether the husband's occupational experience has ever been affected by illness or disability; the number of times the

5   Walter Miller (1968), op. cit.

husband has been unemployed since marriage and the duration of unemployment; respondents' feelings of deprivation).

(1) *Background factors*

The first experience considered was whether or not the husband or wife came from an economically deprived home background. The effects of an economically deprived home upon children can be various. For example, a recent study of disadvantaged children has listed among other things the fact that such children are smaller at birth, die more readily and are generally in a poorer condition in infancy than the children born to the more affluent; malnutrition is more prevalent; and 'during the school years they eat irregularly, their health care continues to be almost totally inadequate, their housing is sub-standard, their family income is low, subsistence on public assistance is high and family disorganisation commonplace'.[6]

In order to simplify our analysis an economically deprived home was defined as one in which the father was in an unskilled occupation, was unemployed, or where there was no male head of household[7] when the respondent/husband was aged twelve. (This was an arbitrarily assigned point in the respondent's childhood, but it was felt that to have asked the respondent to cast her mind any further back would have raised insurmountable problems of recall and lack of knowledge, and to have asked about a later period would have taken us beyond the time of greatest influence upon the child's development.) Even so the data should be treated with caution since (a) not all respondents could be expected to know or to remember accurately what their fathers were doing at that time, and (b) the type of home specified above does not *necessarily* involve a situation of deprivation.

However, the results were generally as would have been anticipated, particularly with regard to the backgrounds of respondents' husbands. The proportion of husbands' fathers who were stated as having been in a social class V occupation, unemployed or not present when the husband was a child (including only those for whom such information was available) was three out of ten in group III2, four out of ten in III4+, five out of ten in V2, and as high as nine out of ten in V4+. For wives the differences were less distinct; those coming from a 'deprived' home background (as defined above) were two out of ten in group III2, four out of ten in groups III4+ and V4+, and five out of ten in group V2.

---

6 H.G. Birch and J.D. Gussow (1970), *Disadvantaged Children* (Harcourt, Brace and World, Inc., New York).

7 J. Askham (1969), 'Delineation of the Lowest Social Class', *Journal of Biosocial Science*, vol. 1, pp. 327–35.

The second background factor considered was the number of siblings of the wife and her husband. Coming from a large family is generally seen to affect the child mainly in two ways: in affecting his physical well-being, and his IQ and subsequent educational and occupational achievement. For example it is stated by Tanner that

> 'the number of children in the family exerts an effect on the children's rate of growth and one which is related to socio-economic class. In the less well-off classes there is a clear-cut relationship between the number of children in the family and their height and weight.'[8]

Again there have been many reports[9] showing that the child from the large family does less well in IQ tests and tests of achievement than the child from the small family. There is still controversy over the kind of relationship that exists between IQ and family size. (Is there, for example, a direct relationship between number of siblings and ability to do well in IQ tests, or are there intervening variables which are related to the type of couples who have large families, and which in turn affect IQ?) Nonetheless such a relationship does exist. Table 5.1 shows that for both husbands and wives there was a difference between those who now have two children, and those who have four or more, in the number of siblings they had. (There was very little difference between social class III and social class V for each of the two family-size groups.) Thus wives with only two children had an average of 2.9 siblings, whereas those with the large families had an average of 4.7 siblings. Amongst husbands the pattern was similar, except that the difference between those with two children and those with four or more was less great, the former having on average 3.5 siblings, and the latter 4.5. (It should be mentioned that number of siblings could influence family-building behaviour not only by affecting the situation of deprivation but also by having a more direct influence upon family-size preferences.)

The final background factor considered was whether the respondent and her husband had any further education or training after leaving school. Such experience obviously influences the individual's position in the occupation market. Miller for example considers type of education as one of the clearest

8   J.M. Tanner (1962), *Growth at Adolescence* (Blackwell, Oxford).

9   See, for example, J.W.B. Douglas (1964), *The Home and the School* (MacGibbon and Kee, London); J.D. Nisbet and N.J. Entwhistle (1967), 'Intelligence and Family Size 1949–1965', *British Journal of Educational Psychology*, vol. 37, pp. 188–93; D. Oldman, B. Bytheway and G. Horobin (1971), 'Family Structure and Educational Achievement', *Journal of Biosocial Science*, suppl. 3, pp. 81–91.

Table 5.1 *Number of siblings of respondent and her husband*

	Wives		Husbands	
	Those with 2 children	Those with 4 or more children	Those with 2 children	Those with 4 or more children
	%	%	%	%
None	13	3	4	8
One or two	35	29	38	17
Three or four	29	19	21	29
Five or six	17	19	23	24
Seven or eight	6	14	10	5
Nine or more	—	14	2	17
Not known	—	2	2	—
Mean number of siblings	2.9	4.7	3.5	4.5
Base for percentages	48	42	48	42

distinguishing characteristics of the lower class, saying that they experience

> 'a pattern of educational involvement characterised by little formal schooling or relatively short periods thereof, with primary emphasis on more generalised social and occupational skills rather than advanced and/or specialised training'.[10]

Again, Allison Davis states,

> 'Education, as the underprivileged worker experiences it ... differs from the education of middle-class persons. It differs in its length, in its content, and in its value as a social and economic tool.'[11]

For the wives in this study, it was found that the great majority had had no further education after leaving school, although those in group III2 were more likely than the others to have had some. (A third of those in group III2 had had further education, compared with only one in ten of all other groups.) The type of further education experienced was in almost all cases

10   Walter Miller (1968), op. cit.

11   Allison Davis (1946), 'The Motivation of the Underprivileged Worker', in W.F. Whyte (ed.), *Industry and Society* (McGraw-Hill, New York).

training for clerical occupations — such as shorthand, typing or book-keeping — although a minority went into nursing or had training for a skilled-manual occupation.

For husbands there was of course a clear distinction between those whom we have classified as social class III (skilled occupations for which training is commonly needed) and those in social class V (unskilled jobs for which training is not usually needed). In social class III therefore the proportion of husbands who had either completed an apprenticeship or had some other form of further education or training was 71%, whereas in social class V it was only 11%. There was no difference between those with two children and those with four or more in either class. The types of education or training experienced were almost without exception those of apprenticeship for skilled manual occupations (electricians, bakers, plumbers, joiners, platers, and so on); one had done a teacher training course; and three others had obtained or were working for ordinary or higher certificates of education at a College of Further Education.

Thus in terms of background factors those in social class V were in many ways more disadvantaged than those in social class III (particularly those in social class V who now have four or more children). With regard to number of brothers and sisters however, those who now have the relatively large families — whether in social class III or social class V — were more likely to have grown up in a relatively large family than those who now have small families.

(2) *Occupational experience*

As already stated, it is in occupational experience itself that the crux of the concept of situational deprivation is to be found. As we are interested in the nuclear family rather than the individual, it is thus primarily with the husband's occupation that we are concerned, since he usually provides the major household income. However wives' occupations can be important; firstly their pre-marital occupation may have subjected them to a low income and occupational insecurity (i.e. and thus contributed to the development of lower-working-class orientations); and secondly if they return to work at some stage after marriage, the type of jobs obtained will have a differential impact upon the economic position of the household and upon the care of children (since they vary by wage level, security, and hours and conditions of work). As with men, women in low-skilled jobs are in the weakest bargaining position, they are among the least well paid, and are the most easily replaceable. The wives' jobs both before marriage and since their last child was born were therefore examined.

Wives in groups III2 and III4+ held somewhat higher-status occupations than those in social class V before they got married, but within each class there was also some difference between those now with two and those with four or more children. Those in III2 were more likely to have held non-manual jobs than those in III4+ (six out of ten, compared with four out of ten) and less likely to have been in an unskilled position (one out of ten, compared with two out of ten). Overall those in social class V were less likely than those in social class III to have been in non-manual occupations and more likely to have been in unskilled jobs. However group V2 wives were more likely to have skilled occupations than group V4+ (four out of ten, compared with one out of ten in V4+) and less likely to have been in unskilled jobs (three out of ten compared with four out of ten in V4+).

Approximately half the wives in all groups had worked for some time since the birth of their last child. In terms of the type of job held the difference between the groups was now no longer along class lines but between those with two and those with four or more children: 45% of those with two children had semi-skilled or unskilled occupations, compared with 84% of those with four or more children. Since the interview did not cover reasons for changes of occupation among wives it would be unwise to speculate about the increase in similarity between group III4+ and V4+, and between V2 and III2. It may have occurred as a result of changing orientations towards work, or it may be simply that certain jobs of an unskilled nature are more convenient (for example in their hours of work) for a woman with four or more children, who finds it more difficult than the woman with only two children to work during the day-time.

Turning to husbands' occupational experience, it has already been established what kind of job husbands had at the time of their wives' first delivery (since that was one of the bases for the selection of the sample). However within the Registrar General's social class groupings there are a variety of different types of occupation, since these classes are to some extent groupings of heterogeneous jobs. They were therefore examined in closer detail, to discover whether those with the larger families were more likely to be in certain types of jobs than others (e.g. those which may perhaps be more insecure than others). We found slight differences between the groups. For example those in group III2 were slightly more likely than those in III4+ to be in jobs which require periods of apprenticeship, as opposed to those which although classed as skilled do not require such training (i.e. six out of ten in III2 were in jobs which require an apprenticeship compared with five out of ten in III4+). In social class V the two groups were also very similar, the majority of them being employed in unskilled industrial jobs. However two out of ten of those in V4+ were fishworkers (a job which has often been even more insecure than other unskilled jobs and has been characterised by unpleasant working conditions) whereas there were none in that category in group V2.

Further, one needs to know whether the husband has remained in his social class III or V occupation since the time at which he was classified. His occupation at that time could have been a temporary phenomenon and he may since have changed to a more (or less) highly skilled job. Thus details of occupational mobility add to knowledge of the situation of deprivation of the families studied. (Other studies have related family size to occupational mobility in a more direct way, showing that compared to those who are not mobile the upwardly mobile have smaller families and the downwardly mobile have larger families.[12] Although the reason for the relationship between the two is not clear, some have suggested that effort towards upward mobility reduces the number of children people desire to have, and this increases their success in contraceptive practice. Downward mobility leads to higher fertility because of low motivation to control family size. This study is more concerned with the effects of the outcome of mobility — namely more or less deprivation and insecurity — rather than with the effects of the process of mobility itself. However the hypothesis outlined above could be in agreement with the present argument, in that the motivation to control family size *and* the desire for occupational mobility could both be affected by similar types of orientation towards life.)

The present concern is whether there has been an increase or a decrease in deprivation (as indicated by husband's occupation) since family-building began. Table 5.2 therefore compares occupation at time of first delivery with that at interview. It should be borne in mind that the period of time covered is only approximately ten years. However some change has taken place; the table shows that although the majority of those in social class III have remained in that occupational class, somewhat more of those in III4+ have been downwardly mobile to less skilled jobs than those in III2 (20% compared with 6%). For social class V also, those with the smaller families have been more successful in occupational terms than those with the larger families: 50% of the former have moved to somewhat more skilled jobs, compared with 30% of the latter. (Later in this chapter we shall examine those in social class V who have been upwardly mobile, and those in social class III who have been downwardly mobile, to see to what extent they

12   See, for example, P.M. Blau and O.D. Duncan (1967), *The American Occupational Structure* (Wiley, New York); C.F. Westoff, R.G. Potter, P.C. Sagi and E.G. Mishler (1961), *Family Growth in Metropolitan America* (Princeton University Press).

Table 5.2 *Husband's occupational class* at time of interview (by occupation at time of first delivery)*

	III2 %	III4+ %	V2 %	V4+ %
Occupation at interview				
— Social classes I–III (non-manual)	7	8	5	—
— Social class III (skilled manual)	87	72	17	12
— Social class IV (semi-skilled)	3	8	28	18
— Social class V (unskilled)	3	12	50	70

* Registrar General's classification

possess in other respects the situational attributes and the orientations of the lower working class.)

To summarise the situation with regard to work experience, again it can be seen that those in social class V were on the whole more disadvantaged than those in social class III, although within each class those with two children have fared better than those with four or more.

(3) *Consequent factors*

A factor which it has been suggested is related to work experience is that of the incidence of illness or disability, which affects the lower working class to a greater extent than others.[13] For example the General Household Survey[14] found that unskilled men of working age reported higher rates of long-standing (or chronic) sickness than all other occupational classes, and that they also had the highest rate of absence from work due to illness or injury. Thus the average number of work days lost, due to illness or injury, per person per year (for working males aged fifteen or over) was 3.9 for professional occupations, rising to 9.3 for the skilled-manual, 11.5 for the semi-skilled, and then to 18.4 for unskilled occupations.

In this study there was a class difference, and also a difference by family-size group, in the incidence of husbands who at some stage between marriage and the time of interview had been out of work as a result of illness or disability. In social class III, none of the husbands in group III2 had been out of work for such a reason, compared with 20% of those in III4+. In social class

13 See, for example, Allison Davis (1946), op. cit.

14 O.P.C.S. Social Survey Division (1973), *The General Household Survey: Introductory Report* (H.M.S.O., London).

V only one man was reported as having had such experience in group V2 whereas in V4+ the incidence rose to 41%. There was a wide variety of types of illness or disability; one man for example contracted a skin disease and therefore could not continue in his job as a fishworker. He was unemployed for a few weeks and then obtained a job as a labourer. Another man received a knee injury whilst working as a labourer, and was off work for eight months before returning to his previous job. (It should be noted that the men in this study are all relatively young – i.e. mainly in their early thirties. Incidence of illness or disability of course increases with age.)

A second factor consequent upon type of occupation is that of experience of unemployment. As has already been stated, lower-working-class occupations are more insecure than other jobs.[15] Again this study supported such a finding: those in social class V had been unemployed since marriage an average of 1.5 times, whereas in social class III the average was only 0.5 times. There was also a difference between those with two and those with four or more children. Thus those in group III2 had the lowest incidence of unemployment (an average of 0.3 times), followed by III4+ with 0.8 times, then by group V2 with 1.0 times, with V4+ having experienced the greatest number of periods of unemployment (an average of 2.2 times).

The total length of time for which the husband had been unemployed since marriage was also examined (although here one could not expect great accuracy because of problems of recall). Again however there was a similar pattern. For example the proportion reporting that their husbands had been unemployed for a total of more than four weeks since marriage was two out of ten in III2, three out of ten in III4+, six out of ten in V2, and eight out of ten in V4+. Long-term unemployment was particularly high in group V4+; thus no one in III2 had been unemployed for a total of over six months, compared with one out of ten in both III4+ and V2, and five out of ten in V4+.

Therefore social class V families with four or more children have been particularly disadvantaged; the husbands have experienced considerably more illness or disability than other groups, they have been unemployed more frequently, and have been out of work for a greater length of time than those in the other groups. Some examples of the kind of experience they have had are as follows:

15   See, for example, N. Bosanquet and G. Standing (1972), 'Government and Unemployment 1966–70: A Study of Policy and Evidence', *British Journal of Industrial Relations* (July), pp. 180–92.

At the time of his marriage the husband was working as a farm labourer, and also working part-time on his own, mending cars. Ever since, he has alternated between labouring jobs and periods of unemployment during which he has augmented his income by mending cars. He said that he would like a permanent job as a motor mechanic, but he has no qualifications.

When he got married the husband was a fishworker. After the first child was born he and his wife and child moved to Grimsby because they had heard that the supply of jobs and the wages were better there than in Aberdeen. They had stayed with relatives, and the husband obtained a job as a labourer in a steel foundry. After a short while however they returned to Aberdeen because they could not find accommodation in Grimsby. After about three weeks' unemployment the husband obtained a job as a bus conductor which he kept for eight years. Then however he got stomach ulcers and had to give up his job. He is still unemployed, and says that his chances of a job are nil at the moment — he cannot go back to being a bus conductor because he drew out all his superannuation when he left and he believes he would have to repay it if he returned.

The husband was a labourer when he got married. He kept this job for two years and then 'fell out with his boss' and was sacked. He was unemployed for about three months and then obtained a job as a road worker. After about three months he began to get pains in his chest and the doctor advised him to try a different job. He was unemployed for a further two or three months and then obtained a job as a labourer with a shipbuilding firm. He retained this job for three years, and then hurt his back at work and had to give it up. He has been unemployed for two and a half years because he was told to take light work only, but 'light work means light pay so he didn't bother'.

Income is another factor that might well be considered in this section. Assessment of a family's income is however a very complex process and involves many and detailed questions to both husband and wife.[16] Unfortunately it was not possible to devote sufficient time to the question of income, nor were husbands interviewed, and therefore — although wives were asked what their husbands' present 'take-home pay' was — it was felt that insufficient response and accuracy of response were obtained for the data to be worth analysing.

16   See, for example, Hilary Land (1969), *Large Families in London*, Occasional Papers on Social Administration, no. 32 (Welwyn).

Finally we may consider respondents' own *sense* of deprivation, for as Cohen and Hodges say, the 'lower-lower class' suffers more than other groups from 'a poverty of resources relative to felt needs and levels of aspiration'.[17] In other words such groups *feel* that they are relatively poor and deprived. This question was considered in the previous chapter and it was found that there was a difference both by social class and by family size in the sense of deprivation. For example, the number of respondents seeing themselves and their husbands as being in the lowest social class was four out of ten in group III2, five out of ten in V2, six out of ten in III4+ and nine out of ten in V4+. Again, when asked what sort of people belonged to their social class, those in group V4+ were far more likely to give answers denoting poverty or deprivation than other groups (e.g. 'those who have a struggle to make ends meet', 'the poor', 'those who haven't enough money'). The proportions giving this type of answer were none in III2, one in ten in V2, two in ten in III4+, and six in ten in V4+.

To conclude this section, the position of the groups with regard to deprivation and insecurity may be summarised as one in which those in group V4+ have experienced a much higher incidence of deprivation than those in group III2 (with groups III4+ and V2 in intermediate positions, although in most cases group V2 is more likely to have experienced deprivation than III4+). Thus the majority of those in group V4+ came from families of five or more children, most of their husbands came from relatively disadvantaged home backgrounds, most of both husbands and wives had no further education or training after leaving school, the majority of husbands have remained in an unskilled occupation during their marriage, and most of them have experienced a certain amount of unemployment. At the opposite extreme, most of the husbands and wives in group III2 came from families of less than five children and had a father who was present and not in an unskilled occupation when they were children, most of the husbands completed an apprenticeship after leaving school (although most wives did not have any further education), and the vast majority have remained in a skilled occupation since their marriage and have experienced either none or very short periods of unemployment since that time.

Those in group III4+ are similar to III2 in that the majority of their fathers − when the respondents were children − were present and not in an unskilled occupation, most of the husbands completed an apprenticeship, and have remained in skilled jobs since they got married. They were unlike III2 in

17   A.K. Cohen and H.M. Hodges (1963), 'Characteristics of the Lower Blue-Collar Class', *Social Problems*, vol. 10, no. 4, pp. 303−34.

having come from somewhat larger families of origin, having experienced more unemployment, and more illness or disability.

Group V2, finally, was similar to V4+ in that the majority of husbands had no further education or training after leaving school, but they were somewhat more likely to have moved since marriage to a more skilled occupation, and somewhat less likely to have experienced unemployment. The husbands were also less likely to have had fathers who were in unskilled occupations, unemployed, or not present when they were children, and also less likely to have come from families of five or more children.

The above findings lead one to ask whether the experience of one type of situation of deprivation or insecurity tends to be accompanied by that of other types. In other words, can the groups be divided into couples with very little experience of deprivation and couples who have experienced deprivation in many different areas, or is the incidence of deprivation more evenly spread throughout the group?

An attempt to answer this question was made by assigning each of the major situations covered in this section a numerical score of either 'nought' or 'one', 'nought' indicating a lack or relative lack of deprivation in that situation, and 'one' indicating the presence of deprivation. For each couple a total score on all situations was then calculated. It should be stressed that this was *not* an attempt to measure quantitatively the extent of deprivation, but merely to show whether or not situations of deprivation and insecurity tend to co-exist.

For this purpose therefore the following were defined as situations of deprivation or insecurity (and thus given a score of one;[18] all other types of experience in each of the areas were given a score of nought). In two cases this entailed the drawing of an arbitrary line between what was and what was not considered a situation of deprivation. In these cases anything below the mean was considered as a situation of deprivation:

(1)   the wife/husband had four or more siblings;

(2)   the wife's/husband's father was in an unskilled occupation, unemployed, or there was no male head of household when the wife/husband was a child;

(3)   the wife/husband had no further education or did not complete an apprenticeship after leaving school;

(4)   the wife was in an unskilled occupation before marriage;

(5)   the husband has remained in an unskilled occupation since he got married (score of 2); the husband has moved from an unskilled occupation

---

18   This is not the case for item (5), which necessitated a three-fold division, and thus a score of 2, 1 or 0.

to a more skilled job *or* has moved from a skilled occupation to a less skilled one (score of 1);

(6) the husband has been unemployed for a total length of time of over one month since he got married;

(7) the husband has been out of work at any time since marriage because of illness or disability.

The lowest score possible was therefore nought, and the highest eleven.

This procedure made it possible to show that situations of deprivation and insecurity do tend to co-exist, particularly for the two extreme groups of III2 and V4+ (see Table 5.3). Thus the proportion of couples obtaining scores of between six and eleven was 3% in III2, 16% in III4+, 33% in V2, and 100% in V4+. (The deviant couples – i.e. those who obtained unusually high or low scores for their group – will be examined in the next chapter.)

Table 5.3 *Number of situations of deprivation or insecurity experienced by the sample couples*

	III2 No.	III4+ No.	V2 No.	V4+ No.
Score				
− 0 or 1	9	3	−	−
− 2 or 3	13	9	2	−
− 4 or 5	7	9	4	−
− 6 or 7	1	4	8	10
− 8 or 9	−	−	4	4
− 10 or 11	−	−	−	3
Mean score	2.6	3.9	5.9	7.7

Two sub-groups from the sample were singled out in order to determine whether they were atypical in terms of the number of deprivations which they had experienced. One was those who though classified as either social class III or social class V at the time of the wife's first delivery[19] have since that time moved into a different occupational category. Therefore, omitting the item of husband's occupation (item 5 above) the mean number of deprivations was again calculated for all groups, and then separately for (a) those social class III husbands who are now in a semi-skilled or unskilled occupation, and (b) those social class V husbands who are now in a more skilled occupation. The

19   This was the stage at which classification into either social class III or social class V was determined.

mean score for each of these categories is shown in Table 5.4.

Table 5.4 *Mean number of situations of deprivation or insecurity experienced (excluding that of husband's occupation)*

	III2 Mean score	No.	III4+ Mean score	No.	V2 Mean score	No.	V4+ Mean score	No.
All couples	2.5	30	3.7	24	4.4	18	6.0	17
Those remaining in social class III/V	2.4	28	3.4	20	4.4	9	5.8	12
Those downwardly mobile from social class III	*	2	5.2	4	–	–	–	–
Those upwardly mobile from social class V	–	–	–	–	4.4	9	6.3	5

* As there were only two persons in this category the mean was not calculated; one had experienced two types of deprivation, the other six.

It might have been hypothesised that within each class the difference between groups was due to the presence of those who through occupational mobility should not have been classified as belonging to that class. However the above table shows that even when the occupationally mobile are removed, the differences between the groups in other types of deprivation still remains. Those who have been downwardly mobile from social class III have experienced more situations of deprivation than those who have remained in social class III. Yet in social class V the converse does not hold: those who have moved to more skilled occupations have not experienced a smaller number of deprivations (apart from occupation) than those who have remained in social class V.

Table 5.4 also shows that those who have been downwardly mobile from group III4+ have experienced on average almost one more situation of deprivation than those in group V2. The question of the overall difference between group III4+ and V2 in extent of deprivation needs comment. For if it is being suggested that the individuals who have experienced most deprivation or insecurity will develop certain types of orientation (which will in turn affect family-building behaviour) then one might expect group III4+ to have had more experience of deprivation than group V2 (since they have larger families). This was however not the case, except for the downwardly mobile. The majority had had less experience of deprivation than those in the unskilled occupations. Yet when types of orientation are examined it will be shown that those in group III4+ are more likely to have developed a lower-working-class outlook than those in group V2. It may be that their relative deprivation compared with group III2 (and V2's relative lack of deprivation compared with V4+) affects the types of orientations which they develop. It will also be shown that for the two intermediate groups of III4+ and V2 there are a minority of couples for whom the thesis of this study does not apply (for example those who have lower-working-class orientations but small families), and for whom a different type of explanation of family-building behaviour must be sought.

Turning again to the number of situations of deprivation experienced, a second factor — apart from that of occupational mobility — which may have influenced the differences between the four groups is that of sub-fecundity; some women may have small families not because they lack lower-working-class orientations but because they are sub-fecund. One would therefore expect that, without the relatively sub-fecund the differences between those with only two and those with four or more children would be even greater. Such analysis shows that those classified as relatively sub-fecund[20] were somewhat more likely to have experienced situations of deprivation than others, but the differences were not great; the mean number of situations of deprivation in III2 was 2.8 for the sub-fecund and for the remainder 2.6; in group V2 the mean was 6.2 for the sub-fecund and 5.8 for the remainder. However these figures should be treated with caution since the study was not able to provide an adequate measure of fecundity or sub-fecundity.

Orientations as Expressed in Patterns of Behaviour
In the previous chapter four general types of lower-working-class orientation towards social action were discussed and related to values, norms, beliefs and goals. This section will consider the extent to which such orientations guide the behaviour of the groups studied, whether or not they are normatively, or otherwise, reinforced.

Many different types of behaviour could have been considered in this context. Since only a few could be examined in this project, a selection was made of the types of behaviour which appeared most relevant in a discussion of family life and fertility behaviour.

It should be stressed that most of the kinds of behaviour considered could not be seen as involving only one of the types of orientation, but often two

---

20   For an explanation of how the distinction between the fecund and sub-fecund was drawn see Chapter 1.

or three. For example an action could involve a present-time orientation plus a lack of concern with material well-being.

The section begins with behaviour which occurred before the birth of the first child, and then considers that which took place later on during the marriage.

(1) *Behaviour before the birth of the first child*

The behaviour with which we are concerned at this stage is that involving events leading up to marriage and the start of married life. This involves the length of time the couple went out together before marriage; how old they were at that time; why they got married when they did; and the kind of accommodation they obtained when they got married. Such behaviour can involve different types of orientation, in that marriage can be seen as an event in which the couple look ahead to the future and make arrangements and plans for the way they would like their lives as a married couple to be organised. It can involve plans or actions showing that certain material standards are considered necessary both for the marriage ceremony itself (for example in the form of wedding garments or the wedding reception) or for the establishment of a home (for example in the form of finding satisfactory accommodation, furniture, etc.). On the other hand, marriage can be a relatively precipitate event in which orientations are towards the present rather than the future, in which few or no plans are made, and in which the material aspects of the ceremony and future accommodation, etc., are not taken into account.

First of all a couple takes a decision to get married, and then a decision to get married at a certain time. It was impossible to examine the decision-making process itself, but there are certain kinds of behaviour which can indicate the types of orientations involved in the process. In the first place there is the length of time for which the couple went out together before they got married. One would expect those with a present-time orientation and those who do not plan their lives to have 'been out together' for a shorter period of time than others. Thus one would expect differences between those who now have two children and those who have four or more. A clear difference was found between groups III2 and V4+, but there was very little difference between the other two groups, who were in an intermediate position. Thus two-thirds of the respondents in III2 said they went out together for over two years before getting married, compared with one-third of those in III4+ and V2, and only a quarter of those in V4+ (see Table 5.5). The mean length of time for each group was 2.4 years for III2, 1.8 years for III4+ and V2, and 1.4 years for V4+.

Age at marriage is also a factor which can indicate a particular type of

146

Table 5.5 *Length of time respondents said they went out with their husbands before getting married*

| | III2 | III4+ | V2 | V4+ |
	%	%	%	%
Up to one year	7	20	22	41
Over one year to up to two years	27	48	39	35
Over two years	66	32	39	24

orientation towards the event. To marry young can indicate that the individual does not consider marriage an event which has to be planned or thought about over a period of years, or an event which occurs for example when a man's occupation has become firmly established, apprenticeship completed, or when earnings have risen to support a family adequately. Again therefore one would expect those with the larger families to have married at an earlier age than others. Table 5.6 shows that this is the case, for both husbands and wives; those with four or more children tended to marry earlier than those with only two.

Table 5.6 *Age at marriage*

| | Wives | | Husbands | |
| | Those with 2 children | Those with 4 or more children | Those with 2 children | Those with 4 or more children |
	%	%	%	%
16–19 years	27	50	11	21
20–3 years	54	43	58	58
24–7 years	13	7	25	19
28 years or over	6	—	6	2
Mean age	21.2	19.7	22.9	21.5

Turning now to what the respondent felt were the reasons why she and her husband got married when they did, one may hypothesise that there will be fewer present-time-oriented than future-oriented reasons, and more forward planning among those with two children than among those with four or more. Again this appeared to be the case, particularly when comparing group V4+ with those with small families. Only approximately a quarter of the couples

147

with only two children gave answers which indicated that the marriage had taken place when it did as a result of a precipitous decision involving little or no forward planning. Pregnancy was the most usual reason for marrying at relatively short notice, for example,

> 'I was expecting. If I hadn't been we'd probably have waited and saved up for a bit longer.' (III2)

Home conditions could also precipitate a marriage; for example,

> 'My parents didn't want me to get married, and they didn't like my man coming to the house – I think it was because I was bringing money into the house and they didn't want that to stop. So we thought I'd be better off leaving home and getting married – then they'd have to accept things.' (V2)

However half of those with two children gave reasons which indicated that the marriage took place after a certain amount of planning. The two most common factors taken into account when planning the time of marriage were financial matters and obtaining accommodation. For example,

> 'We set ourselves the target of saving four hundred pounds, and when we reached it we got married.' (III2)

> 'We got a house in the November, and got married the following March, so that it gave us time to get it ready.' (V2)

The only other two factors taken into account were husband's occupational position, and planning the best time for the wedding ceremony itself. For example,

> 'My man went into the army to do his national service, so we waited until he'd finished that.' (V2)

> 'We booked a year in advance for the hotel for the reception.' (III2)

In groups III4+ and V4+ the decision of when to marry was far more often a precipitous one, in which factors external to the couple's wishes forced or hastened the wedding. In group III4+ about half of the reasons were of this nature, and in V4+ as many as four-fifths. Again the most usual reason was pregnancy.[21] (The actual proportions of women pregnant at marriage was 20% in III2, 17% in V2, 36% in III4+ and 59% in V4+.) No other reason occurred as frequently, but occasionally home conditions or occupational situation could precipitate a wedding:

21   See B. Thompson and R. Illsley (1969), 'Family Growth in Aberdeen', *Journal of Biosocial Science*, vol. 1, pp. 23–39.

'His house was overcrowded and so was mine, so we decided we'd get married, and try to get a place of our own.' (V4+)

'I was in a house on my own. My mother was dead and my father was away trawling so I wanted to get married quickly.' (V4+)

'My man was in the forces, and we suddenly heard he might get moved to Aden, so we thought we'd get married first or it might have meant waiting a long time.' (III4+)

Only one out of ten of those with the large families gave reasons which indicated some forward planning on the part of the couple themselves, and as with those in groups III2 and V2, the reasons concerned finance, housing, or occupational situation.

As it has been shown that the question of accommodation is one which can be taken into account when the decision of when to marry is made, it was considered useful to examine the type of housing which couples obtained immediately after they got married. It was hypothesised that those whose orientations were towards the future and towards planning their lives would be more likely to have obtained a place of their own to live in, and that others would be more likely to have to move in with parents, as they had made no provision of their own. (It should also be mentioned that other factors can affect this type of behaviour, such as the couple's income and whether the wife is pregnant, since some landlords do not allow children.) However the expected pattern was observed, with those in groups III2 and V2 being more likely to have had their own accommodation after they got married and less likely to have lived with parents than those in groups III4+ and V4+. Thus the proportion of couples living with parents at that time was 37% of III2, 50% of V2, and 70% of groups III4+ and V4+. This pattern partially supports what Miller says about the housing behaviour of lower-working-class groups.[22] He states that such people tend to allocate only 'limited portions of the material resources and physical energies to enterprises involving the ownership, maintenance and adornment of residential structures and their environs'.

Thus before they had their first child, those with four or more children (and especially those in group V4+) were more likely than others to act in ways which can be interpreted as springing from or being influenced by the lower-working-class orientations of (a) stress upon present rather than future gratification, (b) passive acceptance rather than active control or planning of their lives, and (c) lack of emphasis upon material well-being or advancement.

22   Walter Miller (1968), op. cit.

(2) *Behaviour during marriage*

Continuing with behaviour related to the couple's accommodation situation, one would expect those with lower-working-class orientations to have moved house more frequently than others. Such a pattern is expected, in that those who do not look to the future or feel able to plan their lives would be less likely to consider their long-term housing situation, whereas others − in planning ahead − would be likely to seek a stable accommodation situation which would not necessitate the disruption which moving house can produce. (Moving house can of course also be directly affected by other factors; for example those with large families may need to move more frequently in order to avoid overcrowding, as more children are born.) Others however have seen a relationship between 'planning' and changing of accommodation. For example, Westoff et al. found that 'the proportion of couples who planned both births was significantly higher for those that reported no move since marriage than for those reporting one move or more'.[23]

The expected pattern was observed in this study; for example only one out of ten of those in group III2 had had four or more homes since marriage, followed by V2 with three out of ten, and then by those with four or more children, amongst whom five out of ten had had four or more homes. The mean number of homes was 2.5 for III2, 2.9 for V2, 3.6 for III4+, and 4.0 for V4+. For those with two children a relatively common pattern was that the couple began married life in a one- or two-roomed rented flat, perhaps moved to a slightly larger flat after either their first or their second child had been born, and then eventually obtained a council flat or house. For those with the larger families the pattern was less clear; for example they may have begun by living with one or other set of parents, moved to a rented flat, moved back to relatives, and then obtained a council house. Very few people became owner-occupiers (only ten couples, eight of whom were in group III2). The three major types of accommodation available to them were relatives, privately rented accommodation, and local authority housing. By the time of interview most people (except in group III2) had become council tenants − half of those in III2, three-quarters of those in V2, and all but two couples amongst those with the larger families.

The *reasons* for moving house may also indicate different types of orientation. One would expect those with the more passive approach to their own life situations and who laid less emphasis upon material comfort to have moved when negative rather than positive pressures were put upon them. Others would be more likely to move in order to improve their housing

23   C.F. Westoff et al. (1961), op. cit.

situation. Those which may be classified as positive reasons for moving house are a desire for a bigger or better place or for a place on one's own (rather than sharing with relatives or friends), or the offer of a council house. Negative reasons are, for example, inability to pay the rent, the property being condemned, the owner wanting the tenant out, or family disagreements leading to a move away from relatives. Although it was not in all cases possible to divide respondents' stated reasons for moving from one house to another into either one or other of these types, it was usually possible to determine those which were clearly positive reasons. Such reasons were — as expected — more common among those with two children than among those with four or more. Thus for example the proportion of couples having a positive reason for moving from their first home was seven out of ten in group III2 and V2, five out of ten in III4+ and only four out of ten in V4+. Examples of some of their reasons are:

> 'We managed to get an unfurnished flat, so we could start getting our own furniture together.' (III2)

> 'We managed to get a flat on the ground floor — so I could watch the children when they were out playing.' (V2)

> 'I didn't like living with his [husband's] parents. His mother and I had dreadful quarrels. She spoiled him, and he always took her side in any argument.' (III4+)

> 'We couldn't afford the rent, because I was expecting and I had to give up work.' (V4+)

Although we have stated above that the extent of moving house could be due to the necessity of large families to move as a result of overcrowding (rather than because of a particular type of orientation towards the future and the planning of one's own life), it was only rarely that those in groups III4+ and V4+ gave overcrowding as a reason for moving house.

Turning from accommodation behaviour to that of the husband in his occupation, one may suggest that those with lower-working-class orientations will change their occupation more frequently than others, because they are less apt to plan and less forward-looking. Others might argue that this is purely a class-related phenomenon resulting from the man's level of skill, and would therefore expect it to distinguish between those in social class III and those in social class V rather than between those with large and small families. This may certainly be a contributing factor, but the hypothesis suggested here is that the husbands in groups III2 and V2 are more likely than those in the other two groups to have a relatively stable occupational history, because they are more capable of manipulating their environment so that they

151

obtain relatively satisfactory jobs and are able to retain those jobs (or if they change, do so in order to obtain a 'better' occupation, such as one with better pay, greater security, or with better chances of promotion).

Only change of *occupation* is examined here, for though it would have been useful to look at changes of employer it was considered impossible to obtain relatively accurate data on this subject. (Thompson and Illsley showed how the proportion of husbands changing their employer in the first five years of marriage ranged from 25% of those with one child to 85% of those with five or more.)[24]

In this study the total number of different full-time occupations which husbands had had since they married *was* found to vary by family size; for example, in group III2 only one in ten husbands had had more than two occupations, in V2 the proportion was three in ten, in III4+ four in ten, and in V4+ five in ten. Similarly the average number of occupations was 1.7 in III2, 2.0 in V2, 2.3 in III4+ and 3.1 in V4+.

Also as expected the reasons for changing occupation varied by group; those in groups III4+ and V4+ were much more likely than those with two children to say that their husbands changed their jobs for what may be called 'negative' reasons rather than for the positive reasons of getting a job with better pay, greater security or better promotion prospects. The negative reasons could be divided into five categories: the husband was 'laid off' or made redundant, he was fired, he disliked the job or the work conditions (but did not leave because he had a better job to which to go), he was prevented from continuing in the occupation through ill health or disability, or he was sent to prison. Of all changes of occupation the proportions in each group which were said to be due to negative reasons were 21% in III2, 29% in V2, 51% in III4+, and as high as 75% in V4+. The types of reason given for changes of occupation are listed in Table 5.7. As examples, four cases are cited below:

> At marriage the husband was a crane operator, an occupation in which he remained for five years. By that time he became 'fed up' with the job because, according to his wife, 'there were no prospects there, and it was a dirty job'. He then obtained a job as a van driver for a dry-cleaning firm, and has been in it ever since. (III2)

> When he got married the husband was a builder's labourer, a job which he retained for about a year. Then the chance of a job came up in Glasgow and he thought he would like a change. (There was also a

24   B. Thompson and R. Illsley (1969), op. cit.

Table 5.7 *Reasons given for all changes of occupation*

	Those with 2 children No.	%	Those with 4 or more children No.	%
Positive reasons — improved pay	12		8	
— improved conditions	9		4	
— improved prospects	2	62	–	27
— improved security	2		3	
— combination of the above	5		6	
Negative reasons — laid off/made redundant	7		15	
— ill health/disability	2		15	
— dislike of job or conditions	2	25	14	63
— fired	1		3	
— went to prison	–		3	
Other reasons (e.g. finished national service)	5	13	5	10
Can't remember/don't know	1		3	
Total	48	100	79	100

house available there.) So he became a coal lorry driver, but 'found it very tiring'. After a few months the family returned to Aberdeen and the husband went into car-dealing, on his own, 'which he enjoyed — but there was no money in it'. So he took a six months' engineering course, but afterwards found it impossible to get a job in engineering and so took a long-distance driving job. He kept that job for about five years, during which time he saved in order to start up again as a car-dealer. He is now doing that and, as his wife said, 'enjoying it and making enough money to keep us'. (V2)

At first the husband was a marine engineer. 'There was plenty of over-time because the shipyards were very busy and he brought home good pay.' But after one and a half years of marriage there was a slump in the shipyards and he was laid off. He decided to join the Merchant Navy. However, he disliked being away from home, and left the job after a few months, when his second child was born, because 'he wanted to come home to see his son'. He was out of work for a short while and then obtained a job back in the shipyards as a marine engineer, in which he has remained ever since. (III4+)

When they got married the husband was a labourer in the saw-mills.

153

Then after five years (by which time he had become a fireman-stoker) he 'packed it in — they started calling on him to go into work at 3 a.m. and work long hours. He was really sick — and there was very little money in it.' He managed to get another job — as a builder's labourer — almost straight away. After three years in this occupation he 'was sacked for refusing to do more than he felt he was getting paid for'. After being unemployed for two and a half months he went to work on a car production line in the south of England, and the family will be joining him down there very soon. (V4+)

A very different area of behaviour is that concerning the marital relationship and the incidence of disagreement and temporary breakdown in the marriage. (The incidence of breakdown will be underestimated in this study because only couples who were still living together at the time of interview were included in the sample.) To some extent marital strains can be seen as a more or less direct result of situational deprivation and the consequent worries which they involve. On the other hand marital tension can be seen as a result of the particular types of orientations which couples hold.

Most writers on the lower working class include in their list of typical lower-class behaviour patterns that of marital strain. For example Campbell says that there is relatively widespread marital instability among the poor, with disruption of marital ties nearly five times as common among the poor as among the non-poor.[25] Hollingshead also states that in the south of the United States between 50% and 60% of lower-class families are broken at least once by desertion, divorce, death or separation.[26] He attributes this both directly to their economic insecurity and to the values which develop in such groups. Cohen and Hodges also found that family life was 'more unstable and strife-ridden' in the lower-lower class than amongst other strata.[27] They explained this phenomenon as resulting from the strains developing between husband and wife when both partners feel a need to retain relatively strong links with their respective kin, as a means of protecting themselves against the insecurity and deprivation of lower-class life. In other words, marital strain develops as a result of behaviour which occurs as a means of adaptation to situational factors. While not denying the strength of this hypothesis we would also suggest that marital strain occurs partly as a result of the

25 Arthur A. Campbell (1968), 'The Role of Family Planning in the Reduction of Poverty', *Journal of Marriage and the Family*, vol. 30, no. 2, pp. 236–45.

26 A. Hollingshead (1954), 'Class Differences in Family Stability', in R. Bendix and S.M. Lipset (eds.), *Class, Status and Power* (Routledge and Kegan Paul, London).

27 A.K. Cohen and H.M. Hodges (1963), op. cit.

orientation of the lower working class towards (a) the future and (b) the individual's control over his own life. If behaviour is present-time oriented then the future of the family will not be taken into account in any marital disagreement, and spontaneous emotions will be expressed rather than any control of discord for the sake of future stability. Also, where individuals feel they cannot control their own lives, then their orientation will be towards passive acceptance of discord rather than towards the taking of active steps to promote harmony.

Respondents were therefore questioned about their marital relationship. They were asked first whether they and their husbands had had any disagreements at the beginning of their married life, before their first child was born. At this stage group III2 appeared to differ from the other three groups, for whereas only a quarter of the former admitted to such disagreements, approximately half of all other respondents did so. Disagreements at that time were mainly over money, relatives (particularly when the couple was sharing a house with either the husband's or the wife's parents), or over a number of minor matters where the wife or husband found it difficult to adjust to living together.

Later in the interview respondents were asked whether they and their husbands had ever had any big disagreements during their married life, and whether the respondent had ever thought of leaving her husband. Again group III2 respondents were least likely to consider that they had had any major disagreements, and they were closely followed by group V2, with those in V4+ being the most likely to have had major disagreements. (Two out of ten respondents in III2 reported major disagreements, three out of ten in V2, four out of ten in III4+, and six out of ten in V4+.) Amongst those who had had disagreements the sources of discord were various; they usually concerned money, gambling, unemployment, the children, the husband's or wife's relatives, or the husband being out of the home too much. The following examples show some of the variety of types of disagreement:

> 'We went through a bad patch a few years ago. The lack of room got on our nerves, and we used to quarrel about money and over the children.' (They were living in a two-roomed tenement flat at that time.) (III2)

> 'He used to hoard money and I used to take it and spend it.' (III4+)

> 'It's usually over the bairns – he doesn't see them much, and they play up when he's at home and get out of their routine. Once I walked out on him for a few hours – it was a row over his mother, when we lived with her. She used to interfere over the bairns and he'd take her side.' (III4+)

'We argue over lots of things, like quite recently he threw me out because he thought I'd been lying about where I'd been, when I'd been out for an evening with the girls. I got back late and he threw me out. I went to my mother's with the kids for a week. Then I came back myself and sorted it out. He'd been wanting to ask me back, but he's too proud.' (V4+)

Although fewer respondents had thought of leaving their husbands the pattern was similar to that of disagreement (as was that of couples who had actually separated temporarily at some stage during the marriage). The number of wives who said they had thought of leaving their husbands was one in ten of III2, two in ten of V2, three in ten of III4+, and four in ten of V4+. None of those in III2 said they had actually separated temporarily, compared with a sixth of those in V2, a fifth of those in III4+, and a quarter of V4+. Thus there is some evidence of greater marital tension amongst those with four or more children, particularly amongst those in group V4+.

It would be possible to continue citing evidence of behaviour which, it is suggested, results not directly from a particular constellation of situational factors but from the possession of a certain type of orientation towards areas of social action. Thus, for example, in the previous chapter, three types of behaviour were mentioned which also fit the expected pattern, and can be partly explained in terms of respondents' orientations. Firstly there was the question of whether or not during the interview the respondent at any time mentioned plans which she had made or was making (for holidays, spending, moving house, the children's future, and so on). In the light of the hypothesis that those with four or more children are more likely to see the individual as being unable to plan his life, then one would expect them to be less likely than the other groups to make such plans. This was the case, with nine out of ten in III2 reporting plans, seven out of ten in V2, six out of ten in III4+, and four out of ten in V4+.

Secondly, although the occurrence of the saving of money may be due partly to the income and necessary expenditure of a family it will also be partly due to their possession of the kind of orientation in which the future is considered rather than merely the present. Here there was a great difference between groups III2 and V4+, but group III4+ was slightly more likely than V2 to report saving. (The proportions saving any money were seven out of ten in III2, six out of ten in III4+, five out of ten in V2, and only two out of ten in V4+.)

Thirdly there is the incidence of voting in parliamentary elections, which showed that those with four or more children were less likely to report voting in the last general election than those with only two children. A belief

156

in the lack of influence of the individual upon wider events could have been a contributing factor in this behaviour.

This section has shown that those with four or more children are more likely to act in ways which have been argued as connoting a lower-working-class orientation than those with two children, and that this pattern of behaviour is particularly true of group V4+. Thus those with four or more children married at an earlier age than others, were more likely to have had a pre-nuptial conception, and tended not to have a marriage-date influenced by forward-looking plans; their housing behaviour has been more unstable; their husbands have had more occupations and have left jobs for negative rather than positive reasons; and the marriage itself has been subject to more tension and instability than among those with two children. Conversely those with two children tended to plan ahead for their future married life, they were not precipitated into marriage by such factors as pre-nuptial conception, they have had relatively stable housing situations, husbands have tended to change occupations only when an opportunity of occupational improvement occurred and their marriages have been relatively free from major disagreements and separations.

Of course not all couples have consistently behaved either in accordance with lower-working-class or non–lower-working-class orientations. For example there are likely to be certain areas of action where some lower-working-class couples *could* plan ahead and think of the future. Overall however there was a distinction between those with four or more children and those with only two and a particularly clear distinction between those in groups V4+ and III2.

As was stressed in the section on situations of deprivation and insecurity, one cannot of course provide a quantitative measure of the extent of deprivation, nor can one do so for the types of orientations which guide behaviour. However, one can summarise for each couple the number of areas of action investigated in which their behaviour was in accordance with either lower-working-class or non–lower-working-class orientations. Again it should be stressed that this is a very crude indicator, but it does help to show the extent of consistency of behaviour, and to distinguish those couples whose behaviour deviated from the common pattern of their group.

For each of the areas of behaviour studied therefore a dividing line was drawn between behaviour that appeared to indicate a lower-working-class orientation and that which did not. (In four cases this was a relatively arbitrary dividing point and had to be based on whether behaviour was above or below the mean for all groups). A score of one indicated that the behaviour was classified as springing from a lower-working-class orientation, and a score of nought that it was not so classified. The following patterns of lower-working-class behaviour were distinguished:

(1)   pre-nuptial conception;

(2)   the couple went out together for one year or less before getting married;

(3)   a precipitate rather than future-oriented reason for getting married at a certain time;

(4)   the wife/husband was under twenty years of age when married;

(5)   the couple lived with parents before the wife's first delivery;

(6)   the couple have had four or more homes since they married;

(7)   they had a negative rather than a positive reason for moving from their first home;

(8)   the husband has had three or more different occupations since marriage;

(9)   the wife reported that she and her husband have had major disagreements;

(10)   the couple have temporarily separated at some stage as a result of disagreement;

(11)   the wife did not vote in the last general election;

(12)   the couple are not saving any money;

(13)   the wife reported no instances of plans made or being made.

The lowest possible combined score that could be obtained was therefore nought and the highest fourteen. Table 5.8 shows that (as with situational factors) types of behaviour patterns do tend to co-exist, especially in groups III2 and V4+. In groups III4+ and V2 there is a wider range of variation. However even though there is variation, Table 5.8 shows the expected pattern, with, for example, 90% of group III2 having 0—4 lower-class-oriented behaviour patterns, 56% of V2, 44% of III4+, and only 12% of V4+. Similarly the mean number of lower-class behaviour patterns was 2.1 in III2, 3.8 in V2, 5.5 in III4+, and 7.4 in V4+.

As in the section on deprivation, it was considered useful to examine the results when those who (a) were relatively sub-fecund and (b) were occupationally mobile away from the social class into which they were originally placed were removed from the sample. This analysis was conducted in order to assess whether those who might have been otherwise classified (i.e. did not *really* belong to the group in which they were placed) were distorting the findings.

The first factor — that of sub-fecundity — appears to have very little effect upon the results; those in group III2 who were classed as sub-fecund had a mean score of 2.7 whilst those who were not sub-fecund had a score of 1.8. In group V2 those classed as sub-fecund and those not sub-fecund had

158

Table 5.8 *Number of behaviour patterns consistent with lower-working-class orientations*

Score	III2 No.	III4+ No.	V2 No.	V4+ No.
− None	6	2	3	−
− 1 or 2	12	3	4	2
− 3 or 4	9	6	3	−
− 5 or 6	2	6	5	4
− 7 or 8	−	2	2	5
− 9 or 10	−	5	1	4
− 11 or 12	1	1	−	1
− 13 or 14	−	−	−	1

exactly the same mean scores of 3.8.

The second factor however − that of occupational mobility − was of more relevance. Table 5.9 shows that in social class III, as expected, those who were downwardly mobile were more likely than those who were not to have lower-working-class-oriented behaviour. However in social class V those who were upwardly mobile were somewhat *more* likely than those who remained in social class V to behave in accordance with lower-class orientations. The difference is not great, and could be spurious (but it is a finding which merits further investigation).

On the whole there was a consistent relationship between deprivation and types of behaviour pattern − i.e. the greater the number of situations of deprivation or insecurity the couple had experienced the more likely were they to behave in accordance with lower-class orientations. As in other respects, the greatest amount of inconsistency occurred amongst those in groups III4+ and V2. For example if one treats as consistent those couples whose score on *both* deprivations and behaviour patterns was either above or below the mean score for their group, and as inconsistent those whose score was above the mean on one dimension and below it on another, then the proportion of couples whose scores were consistent was 80% among those in the two extreme groups (III2 and V4+) and 60% in the intermediate groups (III4+ and V2).

In conclusion, this chapter has demonstrated that the couples who experience the greatest amount of deprivation or insecurity (i.e. those in social class V with four or more children) are likely to behave in ways which indicate, or are consistent with, certain lower-working-class orientations

Table 5.9 *Mean number of behaviour patterns consistent with lower-working-class orientations (by occupational mobility)*

	III2 Mean score	No.	III4+ Mean score	No.	V2 Mean score	No.	V4+ Mean score	No.
All couples	2.1	30	5.5	24	3.8	18	7.4	17
Those remaining in social class III/V	1.9	28	4.8	20	3.6	9	7.2	12
Those downwardly mobile from social class III	*	2	8.4	4	–	–	–	–
Those upwardly mobile from social class V	–	–	–	–	4.1	9	8.0	5

* As there were only two persons in this category the mean was not calculated; one had a score or 0 and the other of 11.

(namely with regard to the future, the individual's control over his own life, and material well-being and status). Conversely those who experience the least deprivation or insecurity (namely those in social class III with two children) are least likely to behave in accordance with lower-working-class orientations. These findings lend support to the hypothesis already stated, that family-building behaviour is influenced by the type of orientations held towards areas of social action, and that deprivation or insecurity produces lower-working-class orientations, which in turn lead to the building of large families.

However there are certain deviant groups for whom this explanation will not totally suffice. Those in social class III with large families and those in social class V with small families can to some extent have their family-building behaviour explained in terms of their experience or otherwise of deprivation and the development of the consequent orientations. They are however more heterogeneous than the other two groups; group III4+ for example contains some couples who have had little experience of deprivation, have not developed lower-class orientations and yet have relatively large families, or some who have developed lower-class orientations without experiencing deprivation, and so on. Also, in group V2 there are some couples who have the lower-class orientations, have experienced deprivation and yet have small families. The concluding chapter, as well as summarising the findings of this study and making suggestions for further research, will consider some possible alternative explanations of family size for those deviant cases.

6
Summary and conclusions

In the preceding chapters the differences between couples in social class III with two children and couples in social class V with four or more children have clearly emerged on almost all parameters. The position of the other two groups studied is in general intermediate between the two extremes. The fact that a four-cell sample was selected, providing a two-way control for each of the four groups, has complicated but broadened the analysis. (For example those in social class V having four or more children could be compared with those in social class V having only two children, and with those in social class III having four or more children.) Thus it has been possible to avoid the assumption that the causes of large families are in all respects the same in social class III as in social class V, or in all respects different. This chapter will summarise the major findings of the research for each of the four groups studied, and will examine those respondents for whom the major thesis of this study (i.e. that family-building behaviour differs as a result of differential exposure to deprivation and insecurity, via the intervention of the development of certain types of orientation towards areas of social action) is not applicable. Finally, certain suggestions for further research will be considered, plus the implications of the results of this study for population control policies.

Family-building Behaviour
In the first chapter it was stated that the achieved family size of the couples studied here depends largely upon the extent of use of birth control practices, which in turn depends upon family-size preferences and the ability to use contraception efficiently.[1]

As far as preferences are concerned the differences between groups are on family-size lines rather than social-class lines (i.e. groups III4+ and V4+ are similar, as are groups III2 and V2). Those with four or more children wanted

---

1   See Figure 1.1.

more children than those who only have two, but they were also much more likely to achieve more children than they wanted, because they were unable to control their family size to the number preferred. Thus, at the time after the birth of the second child, 92% of the respondents in groups III2 and V2 wanted between one and three children and only 8% wanted more than that. In groups III4+ and V4+ 60% wanted between one and three children and 21% wanted more than that. The gap became even wider later on, so that at the time of interview approximately 10% of those in groups III2 and V2 said they wanted four or more children, whereas approximately 50% of those in groups III4+ and V4+ did so. However by the time of interview overachievement was also much higher among those with four or more children: 55% of them had achieved more children than they wanted, compared with only 10% of those with two children. Similarly the proportions who had the number of children they felt they wanted at that time (i.e. either the number they desired all together or the number they wanted to date) were 80% in group III2, 72% in V2, 32% in III4+ and 35% in V4+.

With regard to contraceptive behaviour, there were marked differences between groups III2 and V4+, with the other two groups in an intermediate position. Those in group III2 were for example most likely to have known, before marriage, what sexual intercourse involved and how pregnancy can be avoided; they and their husbands were most likely to have talked together about contraception; they started using contraception early in marriage, tended to use the more reliable methods, and were most likely to have found the method which suited them at an early stage, so that they used fewer different methods of contraception all together than other groups.

In group V4+ however the pattern was very different: the women in that group were more likely than those in other groups to have had no knowledge of contraception in the early part of their marriage, and to have been ignorant before marriage of what sexual intercourse involved; husbands and wives rarely discussed contraception with one another; they were less likely than other groups to begin contraceptive practice early in their marriage, and when they did practise it they used the less reliable methods; women were less likely to have used the pill; and finally those now sterilised were less likely to have initiated themselves the request for sterilisation than other sterilised women.

Compared with those with four or more children, those in group V2 were only slightly more likely to have talked with their husbands, when they got married, about contraception, but more of them knew what sexual intercourse involved and what can be done to avoid pregnancy; they were more likely to start using contraception early in their marriage, and to use the more reliable forms of contraception.

162

The fourth group in the study — those in social class III with four or more children — were also in an intermediate position. In terms of contraceptive knowledge, attitudes and practice they were closer to group V4+ than to those who now have two children. They were less likely than those with two children to discuss the subject early in their marriage, and were more likely than other groups to disapprove of contraception (but they were as likely to know about contraception before they had their first baby as those with two children). Fewer of them started using contraception early in marriage, and when they did use it they tended to use the less reliable methods; they were also more likely than other groups to have used several different methods of contraception (as many of them used the pill at some stage in their marriage as those with two children, but they were more likely to have ceased using it because they found it unsuitable). Compared with group V4+ they started using contraception at an earlier stage; and those of them who are now sterilised were more likely than those in group V4+ to have initiated themselves the request for the operation.

Having examined these patterns of opinion and behaviour one may then ask whether they are consistent with the types of orientation towards social action which have been hypothesised as characterising the upper and lower working class. The four orientations studied were orientations towards the future or the unknown, towards the individual's lack of control of his own life, or control by external agencies, towards material well-being and status, and towards the individual's influence upon wider events.

The fourth orientation — that towards the individual's influence upon wider events — appears to have little relevance for family-size preferences and contraception behaviour, except (as stated in an earlier chapter) in so far as individuals' decisions about the number of children they want and the consequent steps they take to avoid overachievement are influenced by concern for societal overpopulation. In this study such feelings were — not unexpectedly — largely absent. The other three types of orientation however are of considerable relevance for family-building behaviour.

Considering, first, orientations towards the future, one would expect that if the lower working class tend not to consider the future, and tend to have a preference for the familiar as opposed to the unknown, then they would not formulate in advance any definite preferences for the number of children they wanted to have, but would delay their opinion until they had had a certain number of children. This however did not appear to be the case amongst this sample: there was very little difference between groups III2 and V4+ in the proportions saying they had ideas about the number of children they wanted, at different times in their marriage. However, as has been argued, one should not place total reliance upon statements of values but as far as possible examine orientations through behaviour itself, for as we have stated, the way people feel they are able to act is often shown more clearly in how they do act than in their reports of how they feel (or felt) they would like to act.

One would expect that the effect of lower-working-class orientations towards the future upon contraceptive behaviour would be mainly two-fold. Firstly, it is likely that those with such orientations would be less likely to use contraception than others or would start using it at a later stage, and possibly only after they have achieved the number of children they wanted. Such behaviour would be expected of people whose present actions are not influenced by possible future occurrences. The expected pattern was observed, with those in groups III2 and V2 using contraception at an earlier stage than the other two groups. (For example 86% of III2 and 72% of V2 were using some form of contraception before they had their second child, whereas in III4+ only 44% were doing so, and in V4+ 35%.) Secondly one would expect those with a fear of the unknown to have greater problems in accepting some of the more efficient methods of contraception (such as the pill and the diaphragm[2]) because they might not understand and would therefore fear what such methods might do to them. This was also found to be the case, with groups III4+ and V4+ having far more difficulty than the other two groups in accepting both the diaphragm and the pill.

That orientation which involves both the individual's lack of control over his own life and the control or care imposed by external forces or agencies is also likely to affect both family-size preferences and contraceptive usage. As far as family-size preferences are concerned, one would expect that those with lower-class orientations — although they may have preferences — would be less likely than others to think that their preferences can be achieved. In other words there will be a tendency for them to believe that they cannot decide how many children they will have, for such matters are beyond their control (for example, 'you have the number you're meant to have'). One would also expect them to be less likely than other groups to discuss preferences with, for example, their husbands; for if they believe that the individual cannot make plans then there is little point in discussing with others what one desires. The first expected pattern was not systematically studied in this project, nor does the information appear to be available elsewhere. The second expected pattern however was observed, in that respondents in groups III4+ and V4+ felt that they had not discussed family-size preferences with their husbands until much later in their married life than those with only two children.

2   See Lee Rainwater (1960), *And the Poor Get Children* (Quadrangle Books, Chicago), 'Contraceptive Practice: Methods and Meanings'.

With regard to the relationship between contraceptive use and orientations towards the extent of individual control, one would expect that lower-working-class orientations would affect behaviour in the following ways: (a) one would expect that those with such orientations would be unlikely to discuss contraception with others — such as their husbands — because they would not feel that individual initiative is relevant in this area, and therefore there is no point in discussion or planning; (b) such people would be unlikely to make attempts to find out about different methods of contraception, because of their passive rather than active attitude towards control of fertility, and one would therefore expect greater ignorance among them than among others; (c) one would expect less efficient use of contraception among those with lower-working-class orientations, because they would have a tendency to believe that whatever one does, 'you have the number of children you're meant to', or 'things never turn out the way you'd like them to'. Each of these patterns was found to exist. Those in groups III4+ and V4+ were less likely than others to talk with their husbands early in marriage about contraception. (For example before the second pregnancy more than 60% of those in groups III2 and V2 said they had discussed contraception with their husbands, compared with only 40% of III4+ and 30% of V4+.) They learned about contraception at a later stage than others and knew fewer methods all together. They also started using contraception later than others, and were less efficient users. It also appeared that those in V4+ were more passive than those in III4+ in the extent to which they were prepared to use their initiative in procuring an abortion or sterilisation. (For example nine out of ten of those in group III4+ felt that they themselves had initiated the request for sterilisation, compared with only four out of ten in V4+.)

Finally one would expect that those with a lower-working-class orientation towards material well-being and status (i.e. those not oriented towards achievement in those areas) would be more likely than others to develop preferences for relatively large families, because the cost of having children and its effect upon their standard of living would not be seriously taken into consideration. One would also expect them to be less efficient users of contraception, as a result of their relative lack of concern for the consequences of achieving a large family. As already stated both these patterns of behaviour received support in this study.

In conclusion therefore the family-building behaviour of those with four or more children (particularly those in social class V) was consistent with the behaviour one would expect of those whose orientations were towards the present rather than the future, towards lack of individual control, and towards lack of achievement of material well-being.

Cultural versus Situational Explanations of Behaviour

Having suggested the existence of certain types of orientation as an explanation of differential family size amongst working-class groups, we then sought support for this suggestion by examining such orientations in a wider context, firstly within the cultural sphere and then within the situational sphere. In other words we wanted to see whether those with the larger families behaved as they did because they are culturally different from those with small families or because their economic and social situation differs and in turn leads to, or is accompanied by, different types of orientation as expressed in typical ways of acting.

Although we were only able to examine a few of their values, norms, beliefs and goals, Chapter 4 shows that the cultural differences between the groups were not great, except with regard to the beliefs about what it was possible for people in certain situations to achieve. Most respondents did appear to value thinking towards the future, did not feel that people ought not to think of it, and did themselves have some ideas for their own and their children's future. Similarly most respondents appeared to value material well-being, had aspirations for themselves and their children, and did not feel people should give no thought to such matters. On the other hand most people did not believe overwhelmingly in the individual's control of his own life, and valued the care of external agencies. They also expressed no great interest in the wider events of their community or society, and wanted little to do with such matters.

It was therefore estimated that cultural factors could not provide an adequate explanation of differences in family-building behaviour.

Turning to situational factors, it was discovered that the two extreme groups (III2 and V4+) were markedly different from one another in the extent of their experience of deprivation and insecurity. Group III4+ had experienced more deprivation than III2, and group V2 less than V4+ (although group V2 was closer to V4+ than was III4+). It was felt that the crux of this situation was to be found in the type and level of stability of occupation held. Surrounding this were antecedent experiences of deprivation and insecurity predisposing to particular types of occupational position, and, on the other side, experiences consequent upon the holding of such an occupation.

Having suggested that differing experience of deprivation would lead to certain types of orientation as a means of adaptation to differing situations, and assuming that such orientations would show themselves in variety of types of behaviour in addition to that of family-building, we then examined distinctions between the four groups in several different areas of behaviour. These related mainly to the event of becoming married, changes of

166

accommodation during marriage, occupational change, and the existence of marital strain.

It was found that in each of these areas there was a difference between those with two children and those with four or more, and a very clear difference between groups III2 and V4+. Those with four or more children — and particularly those in group V4+ — tended to behave in the way one would expect of those with lower-working-class orientations.

Thus the behaviour of those in group III2 showed the greatest degree of stability, planning and thought for the future; couples went out together for a relatively long time before they got married, and the decision to marry was not a precipitate one; they have had only a small number of homes since they have been married, and when they changed their accommodation they did so in order to improve their situation; the husband has had few changes of occupation, and when he did change his job he did so again in order to improve his position; and finally the marriage itself has been relatively stable, and there has been little marital discord.

Group V2 couples were very similar to those in group III2 in, for example, changing their accommodation or occupation relatively infrequently, and only in order to improve their situation. They were however slightly less future-oriented, etc., with regard to the event of marriage, as indicated by the fact that they were slightly younger at marriage, had been out together for a somewhat shorter period, and were more likely to have lived with parents when they first got married.

Group V4+ on the other hand got married when they were relatively young and for reasons which showed that the decision to marry was a precipitate one; they tended to live with parents at the start of their married life; they have had several different homes, and they did not in general move house in order to improve their situation but for more negative reasons; husbands have had more changes of occupation than those in other groups, and their reasons again were negative rather than positive; and finally their marriages have been the least stable, with the majority of couples experiencing serious disagreements with one another.

Group III4+ was in an intermediate position between group V4+ and the other two groups. Thus approximately half of all marriages in this group were precipitate rather than planned; nearly half of the couples moved from their first home for negative rather than positive reasons; approximately half of the husbands changed occupations again for negative rather than positive reasons, and nearly half of the marriages in this group had involved major disagreements.

The above patterns of behaviour lend support to the hypothesis that where deprivation is low, orientations will develop which stress thought for

167

the future, planning of one's life, and concern for material achievement. Where deprivation is extensive the type of orientations which develop, and which guide behaviour, are a concern with the present rather than the future, a sense of the individual's lack of control over his own life and therefore a passive acceptance of events rather than use of individual initiative, and a relative lack of striving for material achievement. In groups where deprivation is neither absent nor very extensive it is hypothesised that behaviour may have to be explained by other factors, and such cases will be examined further below. On the whole however it is felt that differential family size between social classes III and V can be explained in terms of orientations developed as a means of adaptation to, or recognition of, situational factors.

Profiles of Four Couples
In order to draw together the different areas of investigation studied in the preceding chapters the histories of four couples are outlined below.[3] They were chosen as being relatively typical of their group (without being extreme cases) in terms of their family-size preferences, contraceptive behaviour, orientations and underlying situational experience.

(1)   *The Murdochs (Group III2)*
Mrs Murdoch was born and brought up in Aberdeen. She had no brothers or sisters. Her father was a railway worker. She left school when she was fifteen and worked as a shop assistant until she got married. Her husband had two brothers; his father was a baker, and he himself left school when he was fifteen and served an apprenticeship as a painter. They met at a dance and went out together for two and a half years before getting married. When they married they found an unfurnished rented flat where they have remained (now owning the property) ever since. Mr Murdoch has had a job as a painter ever since they have been married. He is well content with his occupation, according to his wife, and so is she ('as long as he's happy', she added). Neither of them would want to leave Aberdeen even if they got the chance of a better job elsewhere — 'it's family ties that would make us stay'. Mrs Murdoch has not worked since she was expecting her first child and does not think she will do so while the children are at school.

She feels that they are both people who take life as it comes. They have never had any serious disagreements. 'My husband's very easy-going and happy-go-lucky', she said, 'but you can turn to him in a crisis. I'm more quick-tempered, but I'm not a worrier.' She feels that they are in an

---

3   All the names used here are fictitious.

intermediate social class — 'people who work hard and have got all they want'. She said that there was nothing they really wanted for themselves. They are saving, but only for holidays. 'I'm not that ambitious — though I would like us to get a council house.' She is more ambitious for her children — 'I definitely want them to have further education — it counts for a lot these days. I'd like them to go to the varsity — though I'm maybe being too ambitious there. I haven't thought what kind of jobs I'd like them to have — but not painters like their Dad — something with a bit more money.'

When they got married they talked about the number of children they would like and both agreed that they would like three, but that they would wait for a while before having the first in order to 'save up some money to furnish the house'. They practised *coitus interruptus* for eighteen months and then decided that they were ready for the first child. This child — a boy — was born about eighteen months after that. (They wished 'he had come along a bit sooner'.)

Again they discussed the number of children they would like and still agreed that they could afford as many as three. However, they thought they should wait about a year before trying for a second child. They discussed contraception, and Mrs Murdoch asked her doctor's advice. He suggested the pill, which she then took for a few months. However, she forgot to take it whilst they were on holiday, and became pregnant a few months after the first child had been born. They both wished it had not happened quite so soon. 'At first I thought, "Oh dear, more nappies, and two very young children to look after", but there was no need to worry — I managed fine.'

After the second child — also a boy — was born, they still felt they would like to have a third. At the time of interview Mrs Murdoch said she thought they would like to have the third child within the following year or eighteen months. (Since the time of interview this third child — a girl — has been born.) They talked about contraception again, and the GP recommended that she go back on the pill. She did this soon after the second child was born and at the time of interview she was still taking the pill. Mrs Murdoch believes that three children is about the ideal number for the average family and for people like themselves, because 'We couldn't afford to keep more than three, but it's nice to have as many as you *can* afford, because once they get older and are married you've always got your family around you.' You have to realise how many you can afford and plan accordingly. 'It all boils down to money. If I could afford six I'd have six, but nowadays its the poor folk who seem to have loads of kids and can't afford to keep them — young girls who have to get married, and have three kids in five years before they realise.'

(2) *The Mackenzies (Group III4+)*

Mrs Mackenzie was the daughter of a railway worker, who died when she was nine. She had one sister. She left school when she was fifteen, took a shorthand and typing course and had a clerical job. Her husband was the youngest of twelve children. His father was a fish merchant, but spent most of his time in hospital. He also left school at fifteen, and served an apprenticeship in marine engineering. His parents were Roman Catholics but he himself has no religious beliefs.

They met at a dance and went out together for about eighteen months before they got married. The decision to get married at that time was taken because the wife was pregnant. She was eighteen then and he was twenty-two. They lived with Mrs Mackenzie's mother for nearly four years until just before the third child was born and were then offered a council house where they have lived ever since.

Mr Mackenzie, at the time he got married, worked as a marine engineer, but about a year after his second child was born there was a slump in the shipyards and he was 'put on short-time'. He therefore left that job, was out of work for a few weeks and then went into the Merchant Navy. However, when his second child was born (only a few months after he had taken the job) he decided to come home to see his son and so left the Merchant Navy. He was unemployed for a short while before obtaining a job in marine engineering again. He has been in that occupation ever since and is quite content with it, according to his wife. She said that things like promotion were not terribly important to her husband.

She also said, 'I don't think material things mean all that much to me and my husband.' There was nothing that they particularly wanted which they could not afford. Although they made some plans (e.g. for insurance and budgeting) they took other things as they came. Neither did she appear to have strong ambitions for her children – I'd like them to have the best possible education they were capable of, but I wouldn't push them. And I think parents should leave jobs entirely to their children to decide.'

However, even though Mrs Mackenzie felt that she and her husband were not ambitious, she did think that they had plenty of worries. Marriage had been difficult to start with. 'I was very selfish and used to having everything my own way. But we've never had any big rows. My husband's pretty easy-going, though he can be quick-tempered when he's tired. And he's got very definite ideas on certain things, and can be stubborn.' She thinks he worries about the general responsibilities of fatherhood, and that she worries about all sorts of things – 'the children, financial matters, and about dying – I worry about whether there's anything to come after death'. She feels that she and her husband are in the lowest of three social classes – 'We're working class — just ordinary people you come in contact with every day.'

When they got married they talked about the number of children they would like. Mrs Mackenzie wanted about two children but 'didn't think too much about it at that time'; her husband wanted four and his wife said, 'Coming from such a big family it was probably quite a modest size to him.' They did not use any form of contraception before the first child was conceived ('We just thought it couldn't happen to us'), although Mrs Mackenzie did know about the sheath and the diaphragm at that time. She wished she had not had to get married, but her husband was not worried.

After the first child was born they talked about contraception, and the doctor at the post-natal clinic advised Mrs Mackenzie to go to the family-planning clinic, where she was fitted for the diaphragm. They used it for about three months but did not like it, so Mr Mackenzie used the sheath, but during the 'safe period' they were not so careful and so Mrs Mackenzie became pregnant after about six months. She wished she had not become pregnant so soon.

After the second child was born Mr Mackenzie still wanted four children and his wife gradually 'came round to the idea of having three'. They discussed contraception again because the GP advised them to wait for a while before having another child. They decided that the pill would be the safest method, and used it regularly for nearly two years, but then Mrs Mackenzie became frightened of its possible long-term health risk. She stopped taking it and became pregnant almost immediately. However, neither she nor her husband were disappointed. She was then happy with three children but did not want any more. They went back to using the sheath and rhythm method but after about eight months the fourth child was conceived. She was very disappointed but said that her husband was quite happy about it.

She accepted four children but was so exhausted with childbearing that she requested sterilisation. She said she had a fight to get the doctors to agree to perform the operation as she was so young, but eventually they agreed. They are both glad she had it done, as she was so desperate about the thought of having more children. Her husband is glad they have as many as four, but she would have preferred two or three. She thinks four children is a large family. 'People often say to me, "What a shame you've got so many", and that really annoys me — my children don't suffer — they have all they need', but 'about three children is the ideal number of people like us — it's not a big family and it's not a small family and with the present cost of living it's not too big a strain.' When people have four or more children 'in the vast majority of cases they haven't been planned — like me — only one of my pregnancies wasn't unwanted — but people accept it when it happens'.

(3) *The Simpsons (Group V2)*

The Simpsons met at a dance and went out together for two years before getting married. They were engaged for one and a half years. ('My mother would only let us get engaged on condition we waited at least a year.') Mrs Simpson was brought up by her mother as her parents had separated; she had one brother. She left school when she was fifteen and took a shorthand and typing course. She then had a clerical occupation until about a year after she got married. Mr Simpson was the son of a general dealer and had one sister. He had no further education, and had a variety of unskilled jobs.

They got married when Mrs Simpson was twenty-one and her husband twenty-three. She knew what sexual intercourse involved and about the sheath and the diaphragm at that time. They lived at first in a two-roomed furnished flat, but after a year they got the chance of a three-roomed unfurnished flat and are still living there. (Mrs Simpson said she sometimes wished they had stayed in the smaller flat because they would probably have got a council house by now if they had done so.) Mr Simpson worked as a van driver at first, and then at several unskilled jobs, but he was unemployed off and on and was out of work when the first child was born. When the first child was about two and a half years old he got a job as a lorry driver in which he has remained ever since and both he and his wife are quite content with it. She worked full-time in between having her two children, mainly for financial reasons, but has not worked since the second child was born.

She thinks they are ordinary working people, who are content with what they have; they take life as it comes; there is nothing they particularly want, except a council house which they will get eventually. However, Mrs Simpson thinks they would both be willing to leave Aberdeen if her husband were offered a better job elsewhere. He would also like the chance to go on some sort of training course which would improve his occupational position. For her children also she would like 'good jobs – I think education is important. I'd like them to go to university if possible.'

She feels that they had many worries in the early years of their marriage – Mr Simpson had a lot of unemployment, they had money worries, and many disagreements. 'But we're all right now – he has a steady job – and I don't worry so much.'

When they got married they talked about the number of children they wanted and agreed they would like a small family – probably two – 'because it was enough to bring up'. They thought they would like to wait for a while before having the first child in order to save some money 'but in fact we didn't wait very long. It's difficult to explain why, but once we were married we felt that there was something lacking without children.' So they used no form of contraception and were both glad when she became pregnant after about five months of marriage.

After the first child was born neither Mr nor Mrs Simpson wanted any more children for a while. Mrs Simpson did not want to go through the birth again and after that feeling passed they had many financial worries. But when the first child was about four years old they felt financially secure and decided they would like another child. They talked about contraception and Mr Simpson used the sheath except during the 'safe period'. Mrs Simpson said she watched the dates carefully, and this method was used effectively for four years until they decided to give up practising contraception. When Mrs Simpson became pregnant they were both very pleased.

They now feel happy with two children – they discussed it and decided the second would be the last whether it was a boy or a girl. So they have used the sheath again regularly since the second child was born, and intend to go on using it. Mrs Simpson believes that two or three children is the right number for people like themselves, 'because if you've too many you can't give them the individual attention they need'.

(4)   The Anguses (Group V4+)

The Anguses were both born and brought up in Aberdeen. Mrs Angus' father was a labourer, and she had five brothers and sisters. She left school at fifteen and had a job as a fishworker. Mr Angus' father was a stonemason, and he had only one sister. He also left school at fifteen and had a labouring job. They went out together for about eight months and then got married because Mrs Angus was pregnant. She was seventeen at the time and her husband nineteen.

At first they lived with one of Mrs Angus' sisters and then moved to her parents' home because they did not get on very well with the sister and her family. After the first child was born, they acquired a one-room rented flat where they remained until they were offered a council house after the second child was born. After the fourth child was born they moved to a bigger council house.

Mr Angus started his married life as a gardener's labourer. He moved to different firms and experienced several periods of unemployment. He also worked in the fish trade and as a builder's labourer. He has recently obtained a job as a machinist which pays well, but which he finds boring and does not like. However, 'he has no trade so he doesn't think about trying to change to a better job'.

Mrs Angus feels that there are two social classes, and that she and her husband are in the 'low' as opposed to the 'high' class. They have to take things as they come because 'in the position we're in you can't make plans'. She feels that there are plenty of things she would like but cannot afford –

173

'like new furniture, and clothes for the kids'. She says that she is a born worrier, but her husband is 'happy-go-lucky. He's nervous but he doesn't let things worry him.' They have had plenty of disagreements — usually over the children ('My husband says I molly-coddle them').

When they got married the Anguses talked about having children but not about the number they would like. Mrs Angus said, 'We just thought we'd take them as they came.' She thought she would like her children spaced close together so that she would not be old when they were growing up.

They used no form of contraception before the first six pregnancies. The first two children were boys, and the next three pregnancies ended in abortion. The sixth pregnancy led to the birth of a daughter. Before each of these pregnancies they never thought about or discussed contraception because they had no definite ideas about the number of children they wanted, and because Mrs Angus said she thought contraception was 'unnatural'. But after the third child was born — although they still had no definite ideas about the number of children they would like — they talked about contraception because they thought they ought to wait a while before having another child, because of the risk of abortion. So Mr Angus practised *coitus interruptus* for a short while. Then they stopped practising it because they thought they had waited long enough. The fourth child — a second girl — was born eighteen months after the third. Mrs Angus was sterilised after the fourth child was born as the doctor advised it on medical grounds, but she would not have minded another one or two children. Both she and her husband were glad at first that she had been sterilised but 'when Linda grew out of the nappy stage I wished I could have had another baby'. Mrs Angus however felt that four children was really about the right number for people like themselves because 'It's enough to bring up in this day and age as far as money's concerned, but as for looking after them I could cope with more than four. Larger families are happier. A big family tends to be close.'

Alternative Explanations of Family-building Behaviour

This study has advanced the view that the expected pattern of experience and behaviour is either a relatively extensive experience of deprivation, accompanied by lower-working-class orientations and a relatively large number of children; or relatively little experience of deprivation accompanied by non-lower-class orientations and a relatively small family. There are various possible types of deviation from this pattern; for example a couple may have experienced little deprivation or insecurity and yet behave in accordance with lower-class orientations, or they may have experienced considerable deprivation, have lower-class orientations and yet have a small family. The examination of such atypical cases may help to show — by

174

advancing alternative explanations for the behaviour of these couples, which do not contradict the major hypothesis — whether that hypothesis has been well founded.

(1) *Atypical cases amongst those with two children*

Amongst those with small families there were seven clearly atypical cases. Six of these (one in group III2 and five in V2) had experienced considerable deprivation and showed evidence of having lower-working-class orientations. The other couple (in group V2) had experienced much deprivation and yet did *not* appear to have lower-class orientations.

The one couple in the latter category had experienced deprivation in that both husband and wife came from backgrounds in which their families had been in unskilled occupations; the husband had one sister, and the wife eight brothers and sisters. She herself had no further education, and was in an unskilled occupation before marriage. The husband had been in an unskilled job ever since his marriage, and had experienced several months of unemployment. They were however an atypical couple in that they married relatively late (she was twenty-nine and her husband thirty-six when they married). It is felt that this factor may have helped them to break away from lower-class orientations and to develop forward-looking attitudes of planning towards their lives, instead of being hurried into marriage at an early age before stable patterns of behaviour and work experience, etc. could have been developed. It would have been helpful to know more about their lives before marriage in order to confirm this impression, and to find out why they had married relatively late. Another unique characteristic of this couple was that the husband had had a child by another woman some time before his marriage took place, and his wife said, 'He didn't really want any children because he already had one, and if it hadn't been for me we probably wouldn't have had any.'

The other six couples would, according to our hypothesis, have been expected to have relatively large families, in that they had experienced considerable deprivation or insecurity and the accompanying lower-working-class orientations. It was felt therefore that the most likely explanation of their low fertility would be that certain factors intervened to delay or prevent conception or parturition (apart from the couple's own desires or orientations), such as for example infrequent exposure to sexual intercourse, subfecundity of either wife or husband, or a high incidence of abortion.

In five out of the six cases such evidence was apparent. Four out of the six were relatively sub-fecund (i.e. had experienced long periods when no form of contraception was used and yet when they had not conceived). One couple, for example, had in fact had three children by the time of interview;

175

and in the time elapsing between the interview and the writing of this report
another child had been born to them. Their use of contraception had been
minimal: they used no form of contraception until after their third child was
born. The wife was classified as sub-fecund, and it is probable that had this
not been the case the couple would have had four children by the time of
interview and thus have been classified as group III4+.

The fifth couple was atypical in that they have a highly segregated marital
relationship,[4] rarely talking to one another or engaging in joint activities; and
since the second child was born have not, according to the wife, had sexual
intercourse at all. They have never used contraception, and the first two
children were born relatively quickly after marriage.

The sixth couple was unlike the preceding five in that neither sub-fecundity
nor infrequent intercourse could account for their behaviour. For this
couple the explanation seems to lie in fact that they eventually managed to
extricate themselves from a very unstable period in early marriage. They were
married when they were both under twenty, lived with parents, had a number
of disagreements, and experienced many changes of home and of husband's
occupation (he worked as a labourer). It is difficult to explain the change in
approach (the wife herself said, 'We married when we were too young, but as
we got older we settled down'). The husband gave up gambling, their disagreements ceased, and he changed his occupation from labouring to care-
taking because 'he thought labouring wasn't secure enough, and though it
pays well at the moment, he wouldn't be able to make the same money when
he gets older'. This developing attitude of planning for the future also
affected the couple's family-building behaviour: whilst the first child was
pre-nuptially conceived, they have used contraception to space their children
and to limit the number to two.

(2) *Atypical cases amongst those with four or more children*
Nine cases were selected here as being atypical; six of them (all in III4+) had
little experience of deprivation nor did they show evidence of lower-class
orientations; two (both in V4+) had experience of deprivation but had not
developed lower-class orientations; and a further one (in group III4+) had
little experience of deprivation and yet had lower-class orientations.

Those in the first category would have been expected to have small
families. It was felt that the factors which could account for their not fulfilling these expectations would be either factors contributing to exception-
ally high family-size preferences (for example great liking for children which

4   See Elizabeth Bott (1957), *Family and Social Network* (Tavistock, London);
     Lee Rainwater (1960), op. cit.

outweighed any of the perceived costs of a large family), or factors which contributed to difficulty in using contraception (for example religious prohibitions or physical contra-indications to the use of the more efficient methods).

In three of these six cases religion appeared to be an important factor. Two respondents for example were both Roman Catholics (and in one the husband was also a Roman Catholic); in one case the wife said that religion was very important to them and that they went to church every week. Until after their second child was born they used no form of contraception; after that they used the rhythm method ('We never considered any other form because it's against our religion'). Two further children followed, because 'it's not a safe method'. The other Roman Catholic respondent had only ever used the withdrawal method. The third respondent was not a Roman Catholic; she had been brought up in a strict non-conformist religious household, and her religion had influenced her attitudes towards sex, contraception and family-size preferences. For example, she said that when she first got married she thought sexual intercourse 'was dirty – the Bible influenced me a lot – I thought sex was wrong'; and again she said, 'I couldn't really take to contraceptives – I kept thinking about nature and what was meant to happen.' Again – after one pregnancy which occurred as a result of a failure in the use of pessaries – she said, 'I thought God was maybe trying to tell me it was meant to be, that contraception is wrong – and that you have the number of children you're meant to have.'

Two other women with little experience of deprivation and little evidence of lower-class orientations did not have strong religious beliefs, but they were both similar in having a great liking for children, having had difficulty in finding a suitable means of contraception, and having no really strong financial incentives for limiting the size of their families (although they both felt that they had one more child than they wanted: four rather than the preferred three). In one case the husband now owns his own electrician's business and they are buying their own house; in the other the husband has worked as a jetty operator and tanker driver ever since he got married and, as his wife said, 'earns good wages'.

The first couple did not think about the number of children they wanted until after the third was born because 'we both just liked children'. But after the third arrived they felt they had enough to cope with. It was at this stage that problems with contraception occurred. The only method which they both liked – apart from the rhythm method – was the pill. The wife took the pill regularly for about a year, and then became frightened because she had 'had a thrombosis in my leg' and thought it would not be safe to carry on using it. They therefore used the rhythm method, but the wife became pregnant again very quickly. Since the fourth child was born they have continued to use the rhythm method, but 'more carefully this time'.

The second couple talked about the number of children they wanted when they got married. 'We planned to have three — it seemed a nice number, and we both liked children, and with two there's always one that's more spoiled or brighter than the other.' They used the sheath to try to space the first three, and after the third was born still agreed that they wanted no more. They discussed contraception and the wife decided on the pill as it seemed the safest method. She stayed on the pill for about fifteen months, and then came off it 'for a month's rest'. She felt so much better when she was not taking it ('I was less tensed up and irritable') that she decided not to return to it. So she and her husband went back to using the sheath at the most fertile time of the cycle, and withdrawal at other times. This was effective for nearly two years until 'a mistake in the time of the month' led to a fourth pregnancy.

These two respondents can be summed up as women who were strongly motivated towards having children, and who — although they set a limit on the number of children they wanted according to what they felt they could afford or could cope with — had no strong financial worries to curb their preferences (as one would expect such worries to do among those with non-lower-class orientations). They had also both tried the most efficient method of contraception but for certain reasons (fear of the pill or its side-effects) had been unable to continue with efficient contraceptive practice.

The final couple with little evidence of deprivation or lower-class orientations had only wanted two children, but had achieved two more than that number. Their major difficulty had been in finding an acceptable method of contraception. They used no form of contraception before the first child was born, but before the second they used foam tablets for a few months in order to delay the next pregnancy. After the second child had been born 'We said that was enough — we had a boy and a girl — and what with the price of things we couldn't really afford any more.' So they went back to using the foam tablets again, but the wife became pregnant whilst using them ('We always say we don't know where she came from'). After that, 'We thought we'd had our lot, but we weren't so certain now about whether we'd be able to stick at three — as we'd made one mistake we were worried that it could happen again.' The wife went to the Family Planning Clinic, but 'They wouldn't give me the pill at first because I'd had jaundice and high blood pressure. They gave me the coil twice, and it didn't stay in. Then they did give me the pill, but after what they'd said before I was frightened to take them. So we went back to using the foam tablets.' However a further pregnancy occurred. The wife was sterilised after the fourth child was born.

The next atypical case among those with large families was that couple

178

who appeared to have lower-working-class orientations but had experienced little deprivation. What needs explanation therefore is how such orientations developed in the absence of deprivation. It is felt that we had insufficient data on the couple's early life and experiences to answer this question in any sense adequately. The only factor for which there is evidence and which could help to account for their orientations is that both husband and wife seemed to be considerably dependent upon their parents. Both were only children; the wife said that she had 'been brought up very sheltered'; she frequently mentioned the help which both sets of grandparents gave with the children; and often talked about the advice which her mother had given her (for example, in 'nagging' her not to have any more children after the second, and again after the third). It may be that parents provide the kind of support which leads the wife and husband to have passive, dependent, non-planning orientations. However this is a factor which would obviously need a great deal more investigation than we were able to give it in this study.

Finally there were two couples (both in social class V), who had experienced considerable deprivation, but did not appear to have lower-working-class orientations. The questions to be answered here therefore are why it was that they did not have such orientations, and why nonetheless they had large families.

Firstly, both couples – although having experienced deprivation – had managed to achieve considerable stability in their situations, and this may well account for the non-existence of lower-class orientations. The first couple, although coming from considerably deprived backgrounds, had managed to achieve a stable situation since then. The wife was the daughter of an unskilled worker and came from a family of five children. The husband came from a family of seven children, and his father was frequently unemployed. Both left school at fifteen, had no further education, and had unskilled jobs. However they did not marry until she was twenty-two and her husband twenty-four; she was not pregnant; her husband has had only one job in the ten years since they have married, and only two weeks of unemployment.

With regard to the second couple, again the deprivations were all early in life. The wife had ten brothers and sisters (plus another three who died in infancy), and her husband had five (plus one who died). The wife said, 'We're better off than before we were married – we were brought up in poverty.' Also since marriage (which again occurred when the wife was twenty-two and the husband twenty-four, and was not precipitated by pre-nuptial conception) the husband has had only one occupation, and no unemployment. It is suggested that this stability enabled these couples to develop the ability to plan, think of the future and so on.

Secondly, one must therefore enquire why these orientations did not influence family-building behaviour. For in both cases the respondent has achieved more children than she wanted. One had originally wanted two children ('to me that's your family – a boy and a girl'). The other had wanted two or three ('a boy and a girl, but if the first two were both boys or both girls then we'd try again for a third'). The explanation of their behaviour seems to lie in the fact that even though they had been able to develop orientations towards planning etc., in other spheres they had not been able to do so as far as the use of contraception was concerned – both remained scared and 'fatalistic'.

Thus the first couple used no form of contraception before the first two children ('We just didn't think about it'). After the second child was born, she said she thought she might have considered it, but 'I wouldn't ever have gone onto using anything – you hear so many stories – I just didn't fancy it.' When she became pregnant she wished it hadn't happened so soon, but 'you accept it once it happens'. After the third she said, 'I just never got round to it. If you're really determined not to have more family, birth control is a good idea – but I was just the type to let things run.' When she got pregnant again she wished it had not happened at all 'but if it happens, it happens'. At interview she said she was not sure whether they would manage to stop at four children ('You never know – I won't take the steps').

The second couple were also very inefficient users of contraception. For example the wife said that after the third child was born, 'My husband sent me to the Family Planning Clinic, but while I was sitting there waiting I got talking to some women about the cap. They told me how nasty it was, and how horrid it was having it fitted, so I didn't go in. Knowing how unlucky I'd been anyway, there was no point in getting it.'

In conclusion therefore, these atypical cases demonstrate the types of factor which can intervene in the process of situational deprivation leading to lower-class orientations and to a large family, or vice versa. Some couples with considerable experience of deprivation have been able to break away from such a situation in order to achieve a level of stability which has allowed them to develop orientations towards planning ahead, looking to the future, attempts to achieve material well-being, etc. Other couples with little experience of deprivation have not developed non-lower-class orientations, perhaps through excessive dependence upon parents, prohibiting the development of independent, active orientations on the part of the couple themselves. Again, some couples have an unexpectedly small number of children because of sub-fecundity or infrequent exposure to sexual intercourse. Finally others have an unexpectedly large number of children because of either the influence of their religious beliefs (largely upon contraceptive practice) or strong preferences for a large family which are not deterred by financial considerations, or difficulties in the acceptance of the more efficient methods of contraception (such as physical contra-indications, dislike, or fear of certain methods).

Suggestions for Further Research

The findings of this study have certain implications for future fertility studies. Our examination of behavioural practices suggests that merely to examine values, norms and goals as expressed by respondents will be inadequate in the process of explaining differential fertility; the total life situation and the typical ways of acting of different types of couple must also be taken into account. In relation to the concept of family-size preference itself, it is insufficient therefore to ask couples how many children they want to have, intend to have and think they should have (i.e. values, goals and norms); one must also take into account what they believe is a viable way of acting for people in their situation, and what are in fact the typical ways of acting (even though they may not be culturally recognised) of people in different situations.

Although this study has been able to explore a wide variety of factors affecting the achievement of a certain family size, there are many areas of interest and relevance which it was impossible to cover adequately. It also suffered from the disadvantage of being a small-scale study using a small sample of respondents, of involving interviews mainly with the wife only, and being largely a retrospective study of past behaviour and attitudes. It therefore seems appropriate to add a few recommendations for further research in the same field.

The following are some of the major suggestions to emerge from this study:

(1)   a larger-scale descriptive study comparing the incidence of social and economic deprivation with achieved family size, so that sub-samples (particularly of atypical cases) can be identified and more closely investigated;

(2)   further study in depth of specific types of deprivation (for example, unemployment) in order to examine the strategies adopted for adapting to such situations;

(3)   more detailed study of what we have called lower-working-class orientations, to examine their existence in other spheres of action and the extent to which such orientations are recognised by people with different types of social and economic deprivation;

(4)   further studies of values, norms, beliefs and goals as they relate to the four areas of orientation identified in this study;

(5)   a prospective in-depth study of family-building behaviour and any changes in situation and orientation which accompany it;

(6)   studies of husbands as well as wives, in order to examine differences as well as similarities in their orientations, how differences are dealt with, and how the interaction between them leads to or prohibits certain types of action;

(7)   investigations of the social environment within which family-size preferences, and knowledge and attitudes towards contraception are learned and reinforced – for example, the family of origin, the peer group, the work group;

(8)   examination of the transitional period between leaving school and becoming married, in order to discover whether certain types of experience at this stage affect the desire to marry and embark upon the family-building process;

(9)   similarly a study to explore in more detail the reasons why couples get married when they do, and the factors influencing pre-marital sexual behaviour (so that, for example, the implications of differential age at marriage can be explored in detail).

As one of the topics of popular concern at the present time is 'the population problem', it seems appropriate to conclude this report by indicating what implications the findings of this survey have for policies of population control. A high proportion of lower-working-class couples with four or more children do have more children than they would have preferred. However the problem of reducing family size in such sectors of the population is not merely one of finding the most appropriate form of contraception and making it easily available. As this study has suggested, the whole social environment of such couples – in which experience of deprivation or insecurity tends to lead to passive acceptance, inability to plan or to look to the future, etc. – must be taken into consideration. Certain changes will aid in the task of controlling family size – for example, greater ease of access to efficient means of contraception such as can be provided by a domiciliary family-planning service, or the development of a contraceptive without the side-effects and fears produced by the pill. However, an improvement of the economic and social situation of the lower working class is the only certain solution to the problem of family-size reduction for those lower-working-class couples who have more children than they would have preferred.

Appendix

Number of children born since interview
In the time which has elapsed between the completion of interviewing and the writing of this report, twelve additional children have been born to women in the sample. The present number of children in each of the four groups is shown below.

Number of living children

	III2 No.	III4+ No.	V2 No.	V4+ No.
Two children	21	–	14	–
Three children	8	–	3	–
Four children	1	19	1	10
Five children	–	5	–	5
Six children	–	1	–	–
Seven children	–	–	–	2
Mean number of children	2.3	4.3	2.3	4.6

Note: Compare with Table 1.4.

Index of names

Index of subjects